Woman Hating

'One of the world's most notorious radical feminists . . . How refreshing her style of speaking and writing – intoxicating and unapologetic – is compared with the "fun-feminist" prose we see so often on modern bookshelves' *Guardian*

'Dworkin's books do matter. They contain certain truths, of the kind many women recognize as they hear them, about the bewildering ubiquity of sexual violence, the lie this violence gives to the promise of women's equality, and the continuities between the most grotesque aspects of women's treatment at the hands of men and the more quotidian assaults on dignity with which nearly all women are intimately familiar. Dworkin's books speak in a singularly powerful voice: she is one of the more underappreciated prose stylists in postwar American writing. Her books matter too in the more straightforward sense that they have been of real material consequence. Through them, Dworkin helped shape the trajectory of American feminism, giving definitive expression to the radical feminist tenet that sexual domination was the beating heart of patriarchy, and placing the legal battle against rape, domestic violence, sex work and, above all, pornography at the top of the feminist agenda' Amia Srinivasan, *LRB*

'There could be no serious debate on matters such as sexual violence or consent without acknowledging the unflinching courage and originality of her thinking' *Observer*

'Andrea was like an Old Testament prophet. She was always warning about what was about to happen and because of that she was frequently misunderstood. But she also had a breadth and depth of intelligence that was refreshing' Gloria Steinem

'Her dystopian vision of a women's experience dominated at all times by male violence, or the fear of it, could feel like a bold stance against feel-good corporate feminism . . . Dworkin's work leaped off the page' *Jacobin*

'Her writing is a strident and raw look at the systemic bias affecting the everyday experiences of women . . . discomfiting and exhilarating' *The New York Times*

ANDREA DWORKIN

Woman Hating

PENGUIN BOOKS

PENGUIN CLASSICS

UK | USA | Canada | Ireland | Australia
India | New Zealand | South Africa

Penguin Classics is part of the Penguin Random House group of companies whose
addresses can be found at global.penguinrandomhouse.com.

Penguin Random House UK
One Embassy Gardens, 8 Viaduct Gardens, London SW11 7BW

penguin.co.uk

Penguin
Random House
UK

First published in the United States of America by E. P. Dutton & Co. 1974
Published as a Picardor paperback 2025
This edition published in Great Britain in Penguin Classics 2025
003

Copyright © Andrea Dworkin, 1974

Owing to limitations of space, all acknowledgments for permission to reprint previously
published material can be found on page 209.

Drawing on page 88 by Jean Holabird.

Typeset by Jouve (UK), Milton Keynes
Printed and bound in Great Britain by Clays Ltd, Elcograf S.p.A.

The authorized representative in the EEA is Penguin Random House Ireland,
Morrison Chambers, 32 Nassau Street, Dublin D02 YH68

A CIP catalogue record for this book is available from the British Library

ISBN: 978-0-241-73595-4

For Grace Paley

and in Memory of Emma Goldman

. . . Shakespeare had a sister; but do not look for her in Sir Sidney Lee's life of the poet. She died young—alas, she never wrote a word. . . . Now my belief is that this poet who never wrote a word and was buried at the crossroads still lives. She lives in you and in me, and in many other women who are not here tonight, for they are washing up the dishes and putting the children to bed. But she lives; for great poets do not die; they are continuing presences; they need only the opportunity to walk among us in the flesh. This opportunity, as I think, it is now coming within your power to give her. For my belief is that if we live another century or so—I am talking of the common life which is the real life and not of the little separate lives which we live as individuals—and have five hundred a year each of us and rooms of our own; if we have the habit of freedom and the courage to write exactly what we think; if we escape a little from the common sitting-room and see human beings not always in their relation to each other but in relation to reality . . . if we face the fact, for it is a fact, that there is no arm to cling to, but that we go alone and that our relation is to the world of reality . . . then the opportunity will come and the dead poet who was Shakespeare's sister will put on the body which she has so often laid down. Drawing her life from the lives of the unknown who were her forerunners, as her brother did before her, she will be born. As for her coming without that preparation, without that effort on our part, without that determination that when she is born again she shall find it possible to live and write her poetry, that we cannot expect, for that would be impossible. But I maintain that she would come if we worked for her, and that so to work, even in poverty and obscurity, is worth while.

—VIRGINIA WOOLF, A ROOM OF ONE'S OWN (1929)

CONTENTS

ACKNOWLEDGMENT

Ricki Abrams and I began writing this book together in Amsterdam, Holland, in December 1971. We worked long and hard and through a lot of living and then, for many reasons, our paths separated. Ricki went to Australia, then to India. I returned to Amerika. So the book, in its early pieces and fragments, became mine as the responsibility for finishing it became mine. I thank Ricki here for the work we did together, and the time we had together, and this book which came from that time and grew beyond it.

ANDREA DWORKIN

WOMAN HATING

There is a misery of the body and a misery of the mind, and if the stars, whenever we looked at them, poured nectar into our mouths, and the grass became bread, we would still be sad. We live in a system that manufactures sorrow, spilling it out of its mill, the waters of sorrow, ocean, storm, and we drown down, dead, too soon.

. . . uprising is the reversal of the system, and revolution is the turning of tides.
Julian Beck, *The Life of the Theatre*

The Revolution is not an event that takes two or three days, in which there is shooting and hanging. It is a long drawn out process in which new people are created, capable of renovating society so that the revolution does not replace one elite with another, but so that the revolution creates a new anti-authoritarian structure with anti-authoritarian people who in their turn re-organize the society so that it becomes a non-alienated human society, free from war, hunger, and exploitation.

Rudi Dutschke
March 7, 1968

You do not teach someone to count only up to eight. You do not say nine and ten and beyond do not exist. You give people everything or they are not able to count at all. There is a real revolution or none at all.

Pericles Korovessis, in an interview in *Liberation*, June 1973

INTRODUCTION

This book is an action, a political action where revolution is the goal. It has no other purpose. It is not cerebral wisdom, or academic horseshit, or ideas carved in granite or destined for immortality. It is part of a process and its context is change. It is part of a planetary movement to restructure community forms and human consciousness so that people have power over their own lives, participate fully in community, live in dignity and freedom.

The commitment to ending male dominance as the fundamental psychological, political, and cultural reality of earth-lived life is the fundamental revolutionary commitment. It is a commitment to transformation of the self and transformation of the social reality on every level. The core of this book is an analysis of sexism (that system of male dominance), what it is, how it operates on us and in us. However, I do want to discuss briefly two problems, tangential to that analysis, but still crucial to the development of revolutionary program and consciousness. The first is the nature of the women's movement as such, and the second has to do with the work of the writer.

Until the appearance of the brilliant anthology *Sisterhood Is Powerful* and Kate Millett's extraordinary book *Sexual Politics*, women did not think of themselves as oppressed people. Most women, it must be admitted, still do not. But the women's movement as a radical liberation movement in Amerika can be dated from the appearance of those two books. We learn as we reclaim our herstory that there was a feminist movement which organized around the attainment of the vote for women. We learn that those feminists were also ardent abolitionists. Women "came out" as abolitionists—out of the closets, kitchens, and bedrooms; into public meetings, newspapers, and the streets. Two activist heroes of the abolitionist movement were Black women, Sojourner Truth and Harriet Tubman, and they stand as prototypal revolutionary models.

Those early Amerikan feminists thought that suffrage was the key to participation in Amerikan democracy and that, free and enfranchised, the former slaves would in fact be free and enfranchised. Those women did not imagine that the vote would be effectively denied Blacks through literacy tests, property qualifications, and vigilante police action by white racists. Nor did they imagine the "separate but equal" doctrine and the uses to which it would be put.

Feminism and the struggle for Black liberation were parts of a compelling whole. That whole was called, ingenuously perhaps, the struggle for human rights. The fact is that consciousness, once experienced, cannot be denied. Once women experienced themselves as *activists* and began to understand the reality and meaning of oppression, they began to articulate a politically conscious feminism. Their focus, their concrete objective, was to attain suffrage for women.

The women's movement formalized itself in 1848 at Seneca Falls when Elizabeth Cady Stanton and Lucretia Mott, both activist abolitionists, called a convention. That convention drafted *The Seneca Falls Declaration of Rights and Sentiments* which is to this day an outstanding feminist declaration.

In struggling for the vote, women developed many of the tactics which were used, almost a century later, in the Civil Rights Movement. In order to change laws, women had to violate them. In order to change convention, women had to violate it. The feminists (suffragettes) were militant political activists who used the tactics of civil disobedience to achieve their goals.

The struggle for the vote began officially with the Seneca Falls Convention in 1848. It was not until August 26, 1920, that women were *given* the vote by the kindly male electorate. Women did not imagine that the vote would scarcely touch on, let alone transform, their own oppressive situations. Nor did they imagine that the "separate but equal" doctrine would develop as a tool of male dominance. Nor did they imagine the uses to which it would be put.

There have also been, always, individual feminists — women who violated the strictures of the female role, who challenged male supremacy, who fought for the right to work, or sexual freedom, or release from the bondage of the marriage contract. Those individuals were often eloquent when they spoke of the oppression they suffered as women in their own lives, but other women, properly trained to their roles, did not listen.

Feminists, most often as individuals but sometimes in small militant groups, fought the system which oppressed them, analyzed it, were jailed, were ostracized, but there was no general recognition among women that they were oppressed.

In the last 5 or 6 years, that recognition has become more widespread among women. We have begun to understand the extraordinary violence that has been done to us, that is being done to us: how our minds are aborted in their development by sexist education; how our bodies are violated by oppressive grooming imperatives; how the police function against us in cases of rape and assault; how the media, schools, and churches conspire to deny us dignity and freedom; how the nuclear family and ritualized sexual behavior imprison us in roles and forms which are degrading to us. We developed consciousness-raising sessions to try to fathom the extraordinary extent of our despair, to try to search out the depth and boundaries of our internalized anger, to try to find strategies for freeing ourselves from oppressive relationships, from masochism and passivity, from our own lack of self-respect. There was both pain and ecstasy in this process. Women discovered each other, for truly no oppressed group had ever been so divided and conquered. Women began to deal with concrete oppressions: to become part of the economic process, to erase discriminatory laws, to gain control over our own lives and over our own bodies, to develop the concrete ability to survive on our own terms. Women also began to articulate structural analyses of sexist society — Millett did that with *Sexual Politics;* in *Vaginal Politics* Ellen Frankfort demonstrated the complex and deadly antiwoman biases of the medical establishment; in *Women and Madness* Dr. Phyllis Chesler showed that mental institutions are prisons for women who rebel against society's well-defined female role.

We began to see ourselves clearly, and what we saw was dreadful. We saw that we were, as Yoko Ono wrote, the niggers of the world, slaves to the slave. We saw that we were the ultimate house niggers, ass-licking, bowing, scraping, shuffling fools. We recognized all of our social behavior as learned behavior that functioned for survival in a sexist world: we painted ourselves, smiled, exposed legs and ass, had children, kept house, as our accommodations to the reality of power politics.

Most of the women involved in articulating the oppression of women were white and middle class. We spent, even if we did not earn or control, enormous sums of money. Because of our participation in the middle-class lifestyle we were the oppressors of other people, our poor white sisters, our Black sisters, our Chicana sisters—and the men who in turn oppressed them. This closely interwoven fabric of oppression, which is the racist class structure of Amerika today, assured that wherever one stood, it was with at least one foot heavy on the belly of another human being.

As white, middle-class women, we lived in the house of the oppressor-of-us-all who supported us as he abused us, dressed us as he exploited us, "treasured" us in payment for the many functions we performed. We were the best-fed, best-kept, best-dressed, most willing concubines the world has ever known. We had no dignity and no real freedom, but we did have good health and long lives.

The women's movement has not dealt with this bread-and-butter issue, and that is its most awful failure. There has been little recognition that the *destruction* of the middle-class lifestyle is crucial to the development of decent community forms in which all people can be free and have dignity. There is certainly no program to deal with the realities of the class system in Amerika. On the contrary, most of the women's movement has, with appalling blindness, refused to take that kind of responsibility. Only the day-care movement has in any way reflected, or acted pragmatically on, the concrete needs of all classes of women. The anger at the Nixon administration for cutting day-care funds is naïve at best. Given the structure of power politics and capital in Amerika, it is ridiculous to expect the federal government to act in the interests of the people. The money available to middle-class women who identify as feminists must be channeled into the programs we want to develop, and *we* must develop them. In general, middle-class women have absolutely refused to take any action, make any commitment which would interfere with, threaten, or significantly alter a lifestyle, a living standard, which is moneyed and privileged.

The analysis of sexism in this book articulates clearly what the oppression of women is, how it functions, how it is rooted in psyche and culture. But that analysis is useless unless it is tied to a political consciousness and commitment which will totally redefine community. One cannot be free, never, not ever, in an unfree world, and in the course of redefining family,

church, power relations, all the institutions which inhabit and order our lives, there is no way to hold onto
privilege and comfort. To attempt to do so is destructive, criminal, and intolerable.

The nature of women's oppression is unique: women
are oppressed as women, regardless of class or race;
some women have access to significant wealth, but that
wealth does not signify power; women are to be found
everywhere, but own or control no appreciable ter-
ritory; women live with those who oppress them, sleep
with them, have their children — we are tangled, hope-
lessly it seems, in the gut of the machinery and way of
life which is ruinous to us. And perhaps most importantly, most women have little sense of dignity or self-
respect or strength, since those qualities are directly
related to a sense of manhood. In *Revolutionary Suicide,*
Huey P. Newton tells us that the Black Panthers did not
use guns because they were symbols of manhood, but
found the courage to act as they did because they were
men. When we women find the courage to defend ourselves, to take a stand against brutality and abuse, we
are violating every notion of womanhood we have ever
been taught. The way to freedom for women is bound
to be torturous for that reason alone.

The analysis in this book applies to the life situations of all women, but all women are not necessarily
in a state of primary emergency as women. What I mean
by this is simple. As a Jew in Nazi Germany, I would be
oppressed as a woman, but hunted, slaughtered, as a
Jew. As a Native American, I would be oppressed as
a squaw, but hunted, slaughtered, as a Native American. That first identity, the one which brings with it as

part of its definition death, is the identity of primary emergency. This is an important recognition because it relieves us of a serious confusion. The fact, for instance, that many Black women (by no means all) experience primary emergency as Blacks in no way lessens the responsibility of the Black community to assimilate this and other analyses of sexism and to apply it in their own revolutionary work.

As a writer with a revolutionary commitment, I am particularly pained by the kinds of books writers are writing, and the reasons why. I want writers to write books because they are committed to the content of those books. I want writers to write books as actions. I want writers to write books that can make a difference in how, and even why, people live. I want writers to write books that are worth being jailed for, worth fighting for, and should it come to that in this country, worth dying for.

Books are for the most part in Amerika commercial ventures. People write them to make money, to become famous, to build or augment other careers. Most Amerikans do not read books—they prefer television. Academics lock books in a tangled web of mindfuck and abstraction. The notion is that there are ideas, then art, then somewhere else, unrelated, life. The notion is that to have a decent or moral idea is to be a decent or moral person. Because of this strange schizophrenia, books and the writing of them have become embroidery on a dying way of life. Because there is contempt for the process of writing, for writing as a way of discovering meaning and truth, and for reading as a piece of that same process, we destroy with regularity the few serious writers we have. We turn them into comic-book figures, bleed them of all privacy and courage and common sense, exorcise their vision from them as sport, demand that they entertain or be ignored into oblivion. And it is a great tragedy, for the work of the writer has never been more important than it is now in Amerika.

Many see that in this nightmared land, language has no meaning and the work of the writer is ruined. Many see that the triumph of authoritarian consciousness is its ability to render the spoken and written word meaningless—so that we cannot talk or hear each other speak. It is the work of the writer to reclaim the language from those who use it to justify murder, plunder, violation. The writer can and must do the revolutionary work of using words to communicate, as community.

Those of us who love reading and writing believe that being a writer is a sacred trust. It means telling the truth. It means being incorruptible. It means not being afraid, and never lying. Those of us who love reading and writing feel great pain because so many people who write books have become cowards, clowns, and liars. Those of us who love reading and writing begin to feel a deadly contempt for books, because we see writers being bought and sold in the market place—we see them vending their tarnished wares on every street corner. Too many writers, in keeping with the Amerikan way of life, would sell their mothers for a dime.

To keep the sacred trust of the writer is simply to respect the people and to love the community. To violate that trust is to abuse oneself and do damage to others. I believe that the writer has a vital function in the community, and an absolute responsibility to the people. I ask that this book be judged in that context.

Specifically *Woman Hating* is about women and men, the roles they play, the violence between them. We begin with fairy tales, the first scenarios of women and men which mold our psyches, taught to us before we can know differently. We go on to pornography, where we find the same scenarios, explicitly sexual and now more recognizable, ourselves, carnal women and heroic men. We go on to herstory—the binding of feet in China, the burning of witches in Europe and Amerika. There we see the fairy-tale and pornographic definitions of women functioning in reality, the real annihilation of real women—the crushing into nothingness of their freedom, their will, their lives—how they were forced to live, and how they were forced to die. We see the dimensions of the crime, the dimensions of the oppression, the anguish and misery that are a direct consequence of polar role definition, of women defined as carnal, evil, and Other. We recognize that it is the structure of the culture which engineers the deaths, violations, violence, and we look for alternatives, ways of destroying culture as we know it, rebuilding it as we can imagine it.

I write however with a broken tool, a language which is sexist and discriminatory to its core. I try to make the distinctions, not "history" as the whole human story, not "man" as the generic term for the species, not "manhood" as the synonym for courage, dignity, and strength. But I have not been successful in reinventing the language.

This work was not done in isolation. It owes much to others. I thank my sisters who everywhere are standing up, for themselves, against oppression. I thank my sisters, the women who are searching into our common past, writing it so that we can know it and be proud. I thank my sisters, these particular women whose work has contributed so much to my own consciousness and resolve—Kate Millett, Robin Morgan, Shulamith Firestone, Judith Malina, and Jill Johnston.

I also thank those others who have, through their books and lives, taught me so much—in particular, Allen Ginsberg, James Baldwin, Daniel Berrigan, Jean Genet, Huey P. Newton, Julian Beck, and Timothy Leary.

I thank my friends in Amsterdam who were family for the writing of much of this book and who helped me in very hard times.

I thank Mel Clay who believed in this book from its most obscure beginnings, the editors of *Suck* and in particular Susan Janssen, Deborah Rogers, Martin Duberman, and Elaine Markson who has been wonderful to me. I thank Marian Skedgell for her help and kindness. I thank Brian Murphy who tried to tell me a long time ago that O was an oppressed person. Chapter 3 is dedicated to Brian.

I thank Karen Malpede and Garland Harris for their support and help. I thank Joan Schenkar for pushing me a little further than I was willing, or able, to go.

I thank Grace Paley, Karl Bissinger, Kathleen Norris, and Muriel Rukeyser. Without their love and friendship this work would never have been done. Without their examples of strength and commitment, I do not know who I would be, or how.

I thank my brother Mark and my sister-in-law Carol

for their friendship, warmth, and trust. And I thank my parents, Sylvia and Harry Dworkin, for their devotion and support through all these years, which must have seemed to them interminable, when their daughter was learning her craft. I thank them for raising me with real caring and tenderness, for believing in me so that I could learn to believe in myself.

Andrea Dworkin
New York City, July 1973

Part One

THE FAIRY TALES

You cannot be free if you are contained within a fiction.

Julian Beck, *The Life of the Theatre*

Once upon a time there was a wicked witch and her name was

Lilith

Eve

Hagar

Jezebel

Delilah

Pandora

Jahi

Tamar

and there was a wicked witch and she was also called goddess and her name was

Kali

Fatima

Artemis

Hera

Isis

Mary

Ishtar

and there was a wicked witch and she was also called queen and her name was

Bathsheba

21

> Vashti
> Cleopatra
> Helen
> Salomé
> Elizabeth
> Clytemnestra
> Medea

and there was a wicked witch and she was also called witch and her name was

> Joan
> Circe
> Morgan le Fay
> Tiamat
> Maria Leonza
> Medusa

and they had this in common: that they were feared, hated, desired, and worshiped.

When one enters the world of fairy tale one seeks with difficulty for the actual place where legend and history part. One wants to locate the precise moment when fiction penetrates into the psyche as reality, and history begins to mirror it. Or vice versa. Women live in fairy tale as magical figures, as beauty, danger, innocence, malice, and greed. In the personae of the fairy tale — the wicked witch, the beautiful princess, the heroic prince — we find what the culture would have us know about who we are.

The point is that we have not formed that ancient world — it has formed us. We ingested it as children whole, had its values and consciousness imprinted on our minds as cultural absolutes long before we were in fact men and women. We have taken the fairy tales of childhood with us into maturity, chewed but still lying in the stomach, as real identity. Between Snow-white and her heroic prince, our two great fictions, we never did have much of a chance. At some point, the Great Divide took place: they (the boys) dreamed of mounting the Great Steed and buying Snow-white from the dwarfs; we (the girls) aspired to become that object of every necrophiliac's lust — the innocent, *victimized* Sleeping Beauty, beauteous lump of ultimate, sleeping good. Despite ourselves, sometimes unknowing, sometimes knowing, unwilling, unable to do otherwise, we act out the roles we were taught.

Here is the beginning, where we learn who we must be, as well as the moral of the story.

CHAPTER 1

Onceuponatime: The Roles

Death is that remedy all singers dream of
Allen Ginsberg

The culture predetermines who we are, how we behave, what we are willing to know, what we are able to feel.

We are born into a sex role which is determined by visible sex, or gender.

We follow explicit scenarios of passage from birth into youth into maturity into old age, and then we die.

In the process of adhering to sex roles, as a direct consequence of the imperatives of those roles, we commit homicide, suicide, and genocide.

Death is our only remedy. We imagine heaven. There is no suffering there, we say. There is no sex there, we say. We mean, there is no culture there. We mean, there is no gender there. We dream that death will release us from suffering — from guilt, sex, the body. We recognize the body as the source of our suffering. We dream of a death which will mean freedom from it because here on earth, in our bodies, we are fragmented, anguished — either men or women, bound by the very fact of a particularized body to a role which is annihilating, totalitarian, which forbids us any real self-becoming or self-realization.

Fairy tales are the primary information of the culture. They delineate the roles, interactions, and values which are available to us. They are our childhood

24

models, and their fearful, dreadful content terrorizes us into submission — if we do not become good, then evil will destroy us; if we do not achieve the happy ending, then we will drown in the chaos. As we grow up, we forget the terror — the wicked witches and their smothering malice. We remember romantic paradigms: the heroic prince kisses Sleeping Beauty; the heroic prince searches his kingdom to find Cinderella; the heroic prince marries Snow-white. But the terror remains as the substratum of male-female relation — the terror remains, and we do not ever recover from it or cease to be motivated by it. Grown men are terrified of the wicked witch, internalized in the deepest parts of memory. Women are no less terrified, for we know that not to be passive, innocent, and helpless is to be actively evil.

Terror, then, is our real theme.

The Mother as a Figure of Terror

> Whether "instinctive" or not, the maternal role in the sexual constitution originates in the fact that only the woman is necessarily present at birth. Only the woman has a dependable and easily identifiable connection to the child — a tie on which society can rely. This maternal feeling is the root of human community.
>
> George Gilder, *Sexual Suicide*

Snow-white's biological mother was a passive, good queen who sat at her window and did embroidery. She pricked her finger one day — no doubt an event in her life — and 3 drops of blood fell from it onto the snow. Somehow that led her to wish for a child "as white as snow, as red as blood, and as black as the wood of the embroidery frame." [1] Soon after, she had a daughter with "skin as white as snow, lips as red as blood, and hair as black as ebony." [2] Then, she died.

A year later, the king married again. His new wife was beautiful, greedy, and proud. She was, in fact, ambitious and recognized that beauty was coin in the male realm, that beauty translated directly into power because it meant male admiration, male alliance, male devotion.

The new queen had a magic mirror and she would ask it: "Looking-glass upon the wall, Who is fairest of us all?" [3] And inevitably, the queen was the fairest (had there been anyone fairer we can presume that the king would have married her).

One day the queen asked her mirror who the fairest was, and the mirror answered: "Queen, you are full fair, 'tis true, But Snow-white fairer is than you." [4] Snow-white was 7 years old.

The queen became "yellow and green with envy, and from that hour her heart turned against Snow-white, and she hated her. And envy and pride like ill weeds grew in her heart higher every day, until she had no peace. . . ." [5]

Now, we all know what nations will do to achieve peace, and the queen was no less resourceful (she would have made an excellent head of state). She ordered a huntsman to take Snow-white to the forest, kill her, and bring back her heart. The huntsman, an uninspired good guy, could not kill the sweet young thing, so he turned her loose in the forest, killed a boar, and took its heart back to the queen. The heart was "salted and cooked, and the wicked woman ate it up, thinking that there was an end of Snow-white." [6]

Snow-white found her way to the home of the 7 dwarfs, who told her that she could stay with them "if you will keep our house for us, and cook, and wash, and make the beds, and sew and knit, and keep everything tidy and clean." [7] They simply adored her.

The queen, who can now be called with conviction the *wicked* queen, found out from her mirror that Snow-white was still alive and fairer than she. She tried several times to kill Snow-white, who fell into numerous deep sleeps but never quite died. Finally the wicked queen made a poisoned apple and induced the ever vigilant Snow-white to bite into it. Snow-white did die, or became more dead than usual, because the wicked queen's mirror then verified that she was the fairest in the land.

The dwarfs, who loved Snow-white, could not bear to bury her under the ground, so they enclosed her in a glass coffin and put the coffin on a mountaintop. The heroic prince was just passing that way, immediately fell in love with Snow-white-under-glass, and bought her (it?) from the dwarfs who loved her (it?). As servants carried the coffin along behind the prince's horse, the piece of poisoned apple that Snow-white had swallowed "flew out of her throat." [8] She soon revived fully, that is to say, not much. The prince placed her squarely in the "it" category, and marriage in its proper perspective too, when he proposed wedded bliss—"I would rather have you than anything in the world." [9] The wicked queen was invited to the wedding, which she attended because her mirror told her that the bride was fairer than she. At the wedding "they had ready red-hot iron shoes, in which she had to dance until she fell down dead." [10]

Cinderella's mother-situation was the same. Her biological mother was good, pious, passive, and soon dead. Her stepmother was greedy, ambitious, and ruthless. Her ambition dictated that her own daughters make good marriages. Cinderella meanwhile was forced to do heavy domestic work, and when her work was done, her stepmother would throw lentils into the ashes of the stove and make Cinderella separate the lentils from the ashes. The stepmother's malice toward Cinderella was not free-floating and irrational. On the contrary, her own social validation was contingent on the marriages she made for her own daughters. Cinderella was a real threat to her. Like Snow-white's stepmother, for whom beauty was power and to be the most beautiful was to be the most powerful, Cinderella's stepmother knew how the social structure operated, and she was determined to succeed on its terms.

Cinderella's stepmother was presumably motivated by maternal love for her own biological offspring. Maternal love is known to be transcendent, holy, noble, and unselfish. It is coincidentally also a fundament of human (male-dominated) civilization and it is the real basis of human (male-dominated) sexuality:

> [When the prince began to search for the woman whose foot would fit the golden slipper] the two sisters were very glad, because they had pretty feet. The eldest went to her room to try on the shoe, and her mother stood by. But she could not get her great toe into it,

for the shoe was too small; then her mother handed her a knife, and said,

"Cut the toe off, for when you are queen you will never have to go on foot." So the girl cut her toe off, and squeezed her foot into the shoe, concealed the pain, and went down to the prince. Then he took her with him on his horse as his bride . . . .

Then the prince looked at her shoe, and saw the blood flowing. And he turned his horse round and took the false bride home again, saying that she was not the right one, and that the other sister must try on the shoe. So she went into her room to do so, and got her toes comfortably in, but her heel was too large. Then her mother handed her the knife, saying, "Cut a piece off your heel; when you are queen you will never have to go on foot."

So the girl cut a piece off her heel, and thrust her foot into the shoe, concealed the pain, and went down to the prince, who took his bride . . . .

Then the prince looked at her foot, and saw how the blood was flowing . . . .[11]

Cinderella's stepmother understood correctly that her only real work in life was to marry off her daughters. Her goal was upward mobility, and her ruthlessness was consonant with the values of the market place.* She loved her daughters the way Nixon loves the freedom of the Indochinese, and with much the same result. Love in a male-dominated society certainly is a many-splendored thing.

Rapunzel's mother wasn't exactly a winner either.

---

* This depiction of women as flesh on an open market, of crippling and mutilation for the sake of making a good marriage, *is not fiction;* cf. Chapter 6, "Gynocide: Chinese Footbinding."

She had a maternal instinct all right—she had "long wished for a child, but in vain." [12] Sometime during her wishing, she developed a craving for rampion, a vegetable which grew in the garden of her neighbor and peer, the witch. She persuaded her husband to steal rampion from the witch's garden, and each day she craved more. When the witch discovered the theft, she made this offer:

> . . . you may have as much rampion as you like, on one condition—the child that will come into the world must be given to me. It shall go well with the child, and I will care for it like a mother. [13]

Mama didn't think twice—she traded Rapunzel for a vegetable. Rapunzel's surrogate mother, the witch, did not do much better by her:

> When she was twelve years old the witch shut her up in a tower in the midst of a wood, and it had neither steps nor door, only a small window above. When the witch wished to be let in, she would stand below and cry,
> "Rapunzel, Rapunzel! let down your hair!" [14]

The heroic prince, having finished with Snow-white and Cinderella, now happened upon Rapunzel. When the witch discovered the liaison, she beat up Rapunzel, cut off her hair, and cloistered her "in a waste and desert place, where she lived in great woe and misery." [15] The witch then confronted the prince, who fell from the tower and blinded himself on thorns. (He recovered when he found Rapunzel, and they then lived happily ever after.)

Hansel and Grethel had a mother too. She simply abandoned them:

> I will tell you what, husband. . . . We will take the children early in the morning into the forest, where it is thickest; we will make them a fire, and we will give each of them a piece of bread, then we will go to our work and leave them alone; they will never find the way home again, and we shall be quit of them.[16]

Hungry, lost, frightened, the children find a candy house which belongs to an old lady who is kind to them, feeds them, houses them. She greets them as her children, and proves her maternal commitment by preparing to cannibalize them.

These fairy-tale mothers are mythological female figures. They define for us the female character and delineate its existential possibilities. When she is good, she is soon dead. In fact, when she is good, she is so passive in life that death must be only more of the same. Here we discover the cardinal principle of sexist ontology — the only good woman is a dead woman. When she is bad she lives, or when she lives she is bad. She has one real function, motherhood. In that function, because it is active, she is characterized by overwhelming malice, devouring greed, uncontainable avarice. She is ruthless, brutal, ambitious, a danger to children and other living things. Whether called mother, queen, stepmother, or wicked witch, she is the wicked witch, the content of nightmare, the source of terror.

The Beauteous Lump of Ultimate Good

> What can it do? It grows,
> It bleeds. It sleeps.
> It walks. It talks,
> Singing, "love's got me, got me."
> Kathleen Norris

For a woman to be good, she must be dead, or as close to it as possible. Catatonia is the good woman's most winning quality.

Sleeping Beauty slept for 100 years, after pricking her finger on a spindle. The kiss of the heroic prince woke her. He fell in love with her while she was asleep, or was it because she was asleep?

Snow-white was already dead when the heroic prince fell in love with her. "I beseech you," he pleaded with the 7 dwarfs, "to give it to me, for I cannot live without looking upon Snow-white." [17] It awake was not readily distinguishable from it asleep.

Cinderella, Sleeping Beauty, Snow-white, Rapunzel —all are characterized by passivity, beauty, innocence, and *victimization*. They are archetypal good women— victims by definition. They never think, act, initiate, confront, resist, challenge, feel, care, or question. Sometimes they are forced to do housework.

They have one scenario of passage. They are moved, as if inert, from the house of the mother to the house of the prince. First they are objects of malice, then they are objects of romantic adoration. They do nothing to warrant either.

That one other figure of female good, the good fairy, appears from time to time, dispensing clothes or virtue. Her power cannot match, only occasionally moderate, the power of the wicked witch. She does have one physical activity at which she excels — she waves her wand. She is beautiful, good, and unearthly. Mostly, she disappears.

These figures of female good are the heroic models available to women. And the end of the story is, it would seem, the goal of any female life. To sleep, perchance to dream?

The Prince, the Real Brother

> The man of flesh and bone; the man who is born, suffers, and dies — above all, who dies; the man who eats and drinks and plays and sleeps and thinks and wills; the man who is seen and heard; the brother, the real brother.
>
> Miguel de Unamuno,
> *Tragic Sense of Life*

He is handsome and heroic. He is a prince, that is, he is powerful, noble, and good. He rides a horse. He travels far and wide. He has a mission, a purpose. Inevitably he fulfills it. He is a person of worth and a worthwhile person. He is strong and true.

Of course, he is not real, and men do suffer trying to become him. They suffer, and murder, and rape, and plunder. They use airplanes now.

What matters is that he is both powerful and good, that his power is by definition good. What matters is that he matters, acts, succeeds.

One can point out that in fact he is not very bright.

For instance, he cannot distinguish Cinderella from her two sisters though he danced with her and presumably conversed with her. His recurring love of corpses does not indicate a dynamic intelligence either. His fall from the tower onto thorns does not suggest that he is even physically coordinated, though, unlike his modern counterparts, he never falls off his horse or annihilates the wrong village.

The truth of it is that he is powerful and good when contrasted with her. The badder she is, the better he is. The deader she is, the better he is. That is one moral of the story, the reason for dual role definition, and the shabby reality of the man as hero.

The Husband, the Real Father

> The desire of men to claim their children may be the crucial impulse of civilized life.
>
> George Gilder, *Sexual Suicide*

Mostly they are kings, or noble and rich. They are, again by definition, powerful and good. They are never responsible or held accountable for the evil done by their wicked wives. Most of the time, they do not notice it.

There is, of course, no rational basis for considering them either powerful or good. For while they are governing, or kinging, or whatever it is that they do do, their wives are slaughtering and abusing their beloved progeny. But then, in some cultures nonfairy-tale fathers simply had their female children killed at birth.

Cinderella's father saw her every day. He saw her picking lentils out of the ashes, dressed in rags, degraded, insulted. He was a good man.

The father of Hansel and Grethel also had a good heart. When his wife proposed to him that they abandon the children in the forest to starve he protested immediately — "But I really pity the poor children." [18] When Hansel and Grethel finally escaped the witch and found their way home "they rushed in at the door, and fell on their father's neck. The man had not had a quiet hour since he left his children in the wood [Hansel, after all, was a boy]; but the wife was dead." [19] Do not misunderstand — they did not forgive him, for there was nothing to forgive. All malice originated with the woman. He was a good man.

Though the fairy-tale father marries the evil woman in the first place, has no emotional connection with his child, does not interact in any meaningful way with her, abandons her and worse does not notice when she is dead and gone, he is a figure of male good. He is the patriarch, and as such he is beyond moral law and human decency.

The roles available to women and men are clearly articulated in fairy tales. The characters of each are vividly described, and so are the modes of relationship possible between them. We see that powerful women are bad, and that good women are inert. We see that men are always good, no matter what they do, or do not do.

We also have an explicit rendering of the nuclear

family. In that family, a mother's love is destructive, murderous. In that family, daughters are objects, expendable. The nuclear family, as we find it delineated in fairy tales, is a paradigm of male being-in-the-world, female evil, and female victimization. It is a crystalization of sexist culture — the nuclear structure of that culture.

CHAPTER 2

Onceuponatime: The Moral of the Story

Fuck that to death, the dead are holy,
Honor the sisters of your friends.

Pieces of ass, a piece of action,
Pieces.
The loneliest of mornings
Something moves about in the mirror.
A slave's trick, survival.
I remember thinking, our last time:
If you killed me, I would die.

Kathleen Norris

I cannot live without my life.

Emily Brontë

The lessons are simple, and we learn them well.

Men and women are different, absolute opposites.

The heroic prince can never be confused with Cinderella, or Snow-white, or Sleeping Beauty. She could never do what he does at all, let alone better.

Men and women are different, absolute opposites.

The good father can never be confused with the bad mother. Their qualities are different, polar.

Where he is erect, she is supine. Where he is awake, she is asleep. Where he is active, she is passive. Where she is erect, or awake, or active, she is evil and must be destroyed.

It is, structurally at least, that simple.

She is desirable in her beauty, passivity, and victimization. She is desirable because she is beautiful, passive, and victimized.

Her other persona, the evil mother, is repulsive in her cruelty. She is repulsive and she must be destroyed. She is the female protagonist, the nonmale source of power which must be defeated, obliterated, before male power can fully flower. She is repulsive because she is evil. She is evil because she acts.

She, the evil persona, is a cannibal. Cannibalism is repulsive. She is devouring and magical. She is devouring and the male must not be devoured.

There are two definitions of woman. There is the good woman. She is a victim. There is the bad woman. She must be destroyed. The good woman must be possessed. The bad woman must be killed, or punished. Both must be nullified.

The bad woman must be punished, and if she is punished enough, she will become good. To be punished enough is to be destroyed. There is the good woman. She is the victim. The posture of victimization, the passivity of the victim demands abuse.

Women strive for passivity, because women want to be good. The abuse evoked by that passivity convinces women that they are bad. The bad need to be punished, destroyed, so that they can become good.

Even a woman who strives conscientiously for passivity sometimes does something. That she acts at all provokes abuse. The abuse provoked by that activity

convinces her that she is bad. The bad need to be punished, destroyed, so that they can become good.

The moral of the story should, one would think,
preclude a happy ending. It does not. The moral of the
story is the happy ending. It tells us that happiness for
a woman is to be passive, victimized, destroyed, or
asleep. It tells us that happiness is for the woman who
is good — inert, passive, victimized — and that a good
woman is a happy woman. It tells us that the happy ending is when we are ended, when we live without our
lives or not at all.

Part Two

THE PORNOGRAPHY

Among my brethren are many who dream
with wet pleasure of the eight hundred
pains and humiliations, but I am the other
kind: I am a slave who dreams of escape
after escape, I dream only of escaping,
ascent, of a thousand possible ways to
make a hole in the wall, of melting the
bars, escape escape, of burning the whole
prison down if necessary.

Julian Beck, *The Life of the Theatre*

Bookshop shelves are lined with pornography. It is a staple of the market place, and where it is illegal it flourishes and prices soar. From *The Beautiful Flagellants of New York* to *Twelve Inches around the World*, cheap-editioned, overpriced renditions of fucking, sucking, whipping, footlicking, gangbanging, etc., in all of their manifold varieties are available — whether in the supermarket or on the black market. Most literary pornography is easily describable: repetitious to the point of inducing catatonia, ill-conceived, simple-minded, brutal, and very ugly. Why, then, do we spend our money on it? Why, then, is it erotically stimulating for masses of men and women?

Literary pornography is the cultural scenario of male/female. It is the collective scenario of master/slave. It contains cultural truth: men and women, grown now out of the fairy-tale landscape into the castles of erotic desire; woman, her carnality adult and explicit, her role as victim adult and explicit, her guilt adult and explicit, her punishment lived out on her flesh, her end annihilation — death or complete submission.

Pornography, like fairy tale, tells us who we are. It

43

is the structure of male and female mind, the content of our shared erotic identity, the map of each inch and mile of our oppression and despair. Here we move beyond childhood terror. Here the fear is clammy and real, and rightly so. Here we are compelled to ask the real questions: why are we defined in these ways, and how can we bear it?

CHAPTER 3

Woman as Victim: *Story of O*

The *Story of O*, by Pauline Réage, incorporates, along with all literary pornography, principles and characters already isolated in my discussion of children's fairy tales. The female as a figure of innocence and evil enters the adult world—the brutal world of genitalia. The female manifests in her adult form—cunt. She emerges defined by the hole between her legs. In addition, *Story of O* is more than simple pornography. It claims to define epistemologically what a woman is, what she needs, her processes of thinking and feeling, her proper place. It links men and women in an erotic dance of some magnitude: the sado-masochistic complexion of O is not trivial—it is formulated as a cosmic principle which articulates, absolutely, the feminine.

Also, O is particularly compelling for me because I once believed it to be what its defenders claim—the mystical revelation of the true, eternal, and sacral destiny of women. The book was absorbed as a pulsating, erotic, secular Christianity (the joy in pure suffering, woman as Christ figure). I experienced O with the same infantile abandon as the *Newsweek* reviewer who wrote: "What lifts this fascinating book above mere

perversity is its movement toward the transcendence
of the self through a gift of the self . . . to give the body,
to allow it to be ravaged, exploited, and totally possessed can be an act of consequence, if it is done with
love for the sake of love." [1] Any clear-headed appraisal
of O will show the situation, O's condition, her behavior, and most importantly her attitude toward her
oppressor as a logical scenario incorporating Judeo-
Christian values of service and self-sacrifice and universal notions of womanhood, a logical scenario demon-
strating the psychology of submission and self-hatred
found in all oppressed peoples. O is a book of astound-
ing political significance.

   This is, then, the story of O: O is taken by her lover
René to Roissy and cloistered there; she is fucked,
sucked, raped, whipped, humiliated, and tortured on a
regular and continuing basis—she is programmed to
be an erotic slave, René's personal whore; after being
properly trained she is sent home with her lover; her
lover gives her to Sir Stephen, his half-brother; she is
fucked, sucked, raped, whipped, humiliated, and tortured on a regular and continuing basis; she is ordered
to become the lover of Jacqueline and to recruit her for
Roissy, which she does; she is sent to Anne-Marie to be
branded with Sir Stephen's mark and to have rings with
his insignia inserted in her cunt; she serves as an erotic
model for Jacqueline's younger sister Natalie who is
infatuated with her; she is taken to a party masked as
an owl, led on a leash by Natalie, and there plundered,
despoiled, raped, gangbanged; realizing that there is
nothing else left for Sir Stephen to do with her or to her,
fearing that he will abandon her, she asks his permis-

sion to kill herself and receives it. Q.E.D., pornography is never big on plot.

Of course, like most summaries, the above is somewhat sketchy. I have not mentioned the quantities of cock that O sucks, or the anal assaults that she sustains, or the various rapes and tortures perpetrated on her by minor characters in the book, or the varieties of whips used, or described her clothing or the different kinds of nipple rouge, or the many ways in which she is chained, or the shapes and colors of the welts on her body.

From the course of O's story emerges a clear mythological figure: she is woman, and to name her O, zero, emptiness, says it all. Her ideal state is one of complete passivity, nothingness, a submission so absolute that she transcends human form (in becoming an owl). Only the hole between her legs is left to define her, and the symbol of that hole must surely be O. Much, however, even in the rarefied environs of pornography, necessarily interferes with the attainment of utter passivity. Given a body which takes up space, has needs, makes demands, is connected, even symbolically, to a personal history which is a sequence of likes, dislikes, skills, opinions, one is formed, shaped—one exists at the very least as positive space. And since in addition as a woman one is born guilty and carnal, personifying the sins of Eve and Pandora, the wickedness of Jezebel and Lucretia Borgia, O's transcendence of the species is truly phenomenal.

The thesis of O is simple. Woman is cunt, lustful, wanton. She must be punished, tamed, debased. She gives the gift of herself, her body, her well-being, her life, to her lover. This is as it should be—natural

and good. It ends necessarily in her annihilation, which
is also natural and good, as well as beautiful, because
she fulfills her destiny:

> As long as I am beaten and ravished on your behalf, I
> am naught but the thought of you, the desire of you,
> the obsession of you. That, I believe, is what you
> wanted. Well, I love you, and that is what I want too.[2]

> Then let him take her, if only to wound her! O hated
> herself for her own desire, and loathed Sir Stephen
> for the self-control he was displaying. She wanted him
> to love her, there, the truth was out: she wanted him
> to be chafing under the urge to touch her lips and
> penetrate her body, to devastate her if need be . . . .[3]

> . . . Yet he was certain that she was guilty and, without
> really wanting to, René was punishing her for a sin
> he knew nothing about (since it remained completely
> internal), although Sir Stephen had immediately de-
> tected it: her wantonness.[4]

> . . . no pleasure, no joy, no figment of her imagination
> could ever compete with the happiness she felt at the
> way he used her with such utter freedom, at the notion
> that he could do anything with her, that there was no
> limit, no restriction in the manner with which, on her
> body, he might search for pleasure.[5]

O is totally possessed. That means that she is an
object, with no control over her own mobility, capable
of no assertion of personality. Her body is *a* body, in
the same way that a pencil is a pencil, a bucket is a
bucket, or, as Gertrude Stein pointedly said, a rose is
a rose. It also means that O's energy, or power, as a
woman, as Woman, is absorbed. Possession here de-
notes a biological transference of power which brings

with it a commensurate spiritual strength to the possessor. O does more than offer herself; she is herself the
offering. To offer herself would be prosaic Christian
self-sacrifice, but as the offering she is the vehicle of
the miraculous—she incorporates the divine.

Here sacrifice has its ancient, primal meaning:
that which was given at the beginning becomes the gift.
The first fruits of the harvest were dedicated to and
consumed by the vegetation spirit which provided them.
The destruction of the victim in human or animal
sacrifice or the consumption of the offering was the
very definition of the sacrifice—death was necessary
because the victim was or represented the life-giving
substance, the vital energy source, which had to be
liberated, which only death could liberate. An actual
death, the sacrifice per se, not only liberated benevolent
energy but also ensured a propagation and increase of
life energy (concretely expressed as fertility) by a sort
of magical ecology, a recycling of basic energy, or raw
power. O's victimization is the confirmation of her
power, a power which is transcendental and which has
as its essence the sacred processes of life, death, and
regeneration.

But the full significance of possession, both mys-
tically and mythologically, is not yet clear. In mystic
experience communion (wrongly called possession
sometimes) has meant the dissolution of the ego, the
entry into ecstasy, union with and illumination of the
godhead. The experience of communion has been the
province of the mystic, prophet, or visionary, those who
were able to alchemize their energy into pure spirit
and this spirit into a state of grace. Possession, rightly

defined, is the perversion of the mystic experience; it is by its very nature demonic because its goal is power, its means are violence and oppression. It spills the blood of its victim and in doing so estranges itself from life-giving union. O's lover thinks that she gives herself freely but if she did not, he would take her anyway. Their relationship is the incarnation of demonic possession:

> Thus he would possess her as a god possesses his creatures, whom he lays hold of in the guise of a monster or bird, of an invisible spirit or a state of ecstasy. He did not wish to leave her. The more he surrendered her, the more he would hold her dear. The fact that he gave her was to him a proof, and ought to be for her as well, that she belonged to him: one can only give what belongs to you. He gave her only to reclaim her immediately, to reclaim her enriched in his eyes, like some common object which had been used for some divine purpose and has thus been consecrated. For a long time he had wanted to prostitute her, and he was delighted to feel that the pleasure he was deriving was even greater than he had hoped, and that it bound him to her all the more so because, through it, she would be more humiliated and ravished. Since she loved him, she could not help loving whatever derived from him.[6]

A precise corollary of possession is prostitution. The prostitute, the woman as object, is defined by the usage to which the possessor puts her. Her subjugation is the signet of his power. Prostitution means for the woman the carnal annihilation of will and choice, but for the man it once again signifies an increase in power, pure and simple. To call the power of the possessor, which he

demonstrates by playing superpimp, divine, or to confuse it with ecstasy or communion, is to grossly misunderstand. "All the mouths that had probed her
mouth, all the hands that had seized her breasts and
belly, all the members that had been thrust into her had
so perfectly provided the living proof that she was
worthy of being prostituted and had, so to speak, sanctified her." [7] Of course, it is not O who is sanctified,
but René, or Sir Stephen, or the others, through her.

O's prostitution is a vicious caricature of old-world
religious prostitution. The ancient sacral prostitution
of the Hebrews, Greeks, Indians, et al., was the ritual
expression of respect and veneration for the powers of
fertility and generation. The priestesses/prostitutes of
the temple were literal personifications of the life energy
of the earth goddess, and transferred that energy to
those who participated in her rites. The cosmic principles, articulated as divine male and divine female, were
ritually united in the temple because clearly only through
their continuing and repeated union could the fertility
of the earth and the well-being of a people be ensured.
Sacred prostitution was "nothing less than an act of
communion with god (or godhead) and was as remote
from sensuality as the Christian act of communion is
remote from gluttony." [8] O and all of the women at
Roissy are distinguished by their sterility and bear no
resemblance whatsoever to any known goddess. No
mention is ever made of conception or menstruation,
and procreation is never a consequence of fucking. O's
fertility has been rendered O. There is nothing sacred
about O's prostitution.

O's degradation is occasioned by the male need for

and fear of initiation into manhood. Initiation rites generally include a period of absolute solitude, isolation, followed by tests of physical courage, mental endurance, often through torture and physical mutilation, resulting in a permanent scar or tattoo which marks the successful initiate. The process of initiation is designed to reveal the values, rites, and rules of manhood and confers on the initiate the responsibilities and privileges of manhood. What occurs at Roissy is a clear perversion of real initiation. René and the others mutilate O's body, but they are themselves untouched. Her body substitutes for their bodies. O is marked with the scars which they should bear. She undergoes their ordeal for them, endures the solitude and isolation, the torture, the mutilation. In trying to become gods, they have bypassed the necessary rigors of becoming men. The fact that the tortures must be repeated endlessly, not only on O but on large numbers of women who are forced as well as persuaded, demonstrates that the men of Roissy never in fact become men, are never initiates, never achieve the security of realized manhood.

What would be the sign of the initiate, the final mark or scar, manifests in the case of O as an ultimate expression of sadism. The rings through O's cunt with Sir Stephen's name and heraldry, and the brand on her ass, are permanent wedding rings rightly placed. They mark her as an owned object and in no way symbolize the passage into maturity and freedom. The same might be said of the conventional wedding ring.

O, in her never-ending role as surrogate everything, also is the direct sexual link between Sir Stephen and René. That the two men love each other and fuck each other through O is made clear by the fact that Sir Stephen uses O anally most of the time. The consequences of misdirecting sexual energy are awesome indeed.

But what is most extraordinary about *Story of O* is the mind-boggling literary style of Pauline Réage, its author. O is wanton yet pure, Sir Stephen is cruel yet kind, René is brutal yet gentle, a wall is black yet white. Everything is what it is, what it isn't, and its direct opposite. That technique, which is so skillfully executed, might help to account for the compelling irrationality of *Story of O*. For those women who are convinced yet doubtful, attracted yet repelled, there is this schema for self-protection: *the double-double think that the author engages in is very easy to deal with if we just realize that we only have to double-double unthink it.*

To sum up, *Story of O* is a story of psychic cannibalism, demonic possession, a story which posits men and women as being at opposite poles of the universe — the survival of one dependent on the absolute destruction of the other. It asks, like many stories, who is the most powerful, and it answers: men are, literally over women's dead bodies.

CHAPTER 4

Woman as Victim:
The Image

The Image, by Jean de Berg, is a love story, a Christian love story and also a story of Christian love. No book makes more clear the Christian experience of woman after the fall, as we know her, Eve's unfortunate descendant. *The Image*, like the catechism, is a handbook of Christianity in action. In addition, *The Image* is an almost clinical dissection of role-playing and its sex-relatedness, of duality as the structural basis of male-female violence.

It would be an exaggeration of some substance to call the following a summary of plot, but what happens in *The Image* is this: Jean de Berg, the auteur of *The Image*, meets Claire, whom he has known casually for many years, at a party; he has always been interested in her, but her coldness, aloofness, and perfect beauty made her lack the necessary vulnerability which would have made her, in the *veni, vidi, vici* tradition, a desirable conquest; Claire introduces him to Anne, Innocent Young Girl Dressed In White, who, it turns out, is Claire's slave; they go to a bar where Anne is offered to Jean de Berg; they go to a rose garden where Anne sticks a rose by its thorns into the flesh of her cunt;

they go to a restaurant where Claire shames Anne, an event often repeated (Claire shames Anne by ordering her to raise her skirt, or lower her blouse, or by sticking her finger up Anne's cunt); Claire shows Jean de Berg photographs in the artsy-craftsy sadomasochistic tradition for which Anne modeled, except for the last photograph, which is clearly a photo of Claire herself; Claire whips Anne; Anne sucks Jean de Berg's cock; Jean de Berg takes Anne to buy lingerie and humiliates Anne and embarrasses the salesgirl by exhibiting Anne's whip scars which are fresh; Anne is given a bath by Claire in Jean de Berg's presence in which Anne is almost drowned (erotically); it occurs to Jean de Berg that he would like to fuck Claire—which causes Claire to increase the viciousness of her assaults on Anne; Anne is tortured in the Gothic chamber and then ravaged anally by Jean de Berg; Jean de Berg goes home, has a dream about Claire, is awakened by a knock on the door, and lo and behold! Claire has recognized her true role in life (" 'I have come,' she said quietly") [1]— that of Jean de Berg's slave. He hits her, and she lives happily ever after.

Of course, the above is again somewhat sketchy. I did not mention that Anne was forced to piss in public in the rose garden, or how she was nasty to Jean de Berg in a bookstore (a crucial point—since she then had to be punished), or how she fetched the whips herself, or how she was made to serve Claire and Jean de Berg orangeade before they stuck burning needles in her breasts.

The characterizations have even less depth and complexity, not to mention subtlety and sensitivity, than the plot. Claire is cold and aloof. Jean de Berg describes her:

> Claire was very beautiful, as I said, probably even more beautiful than her friend in the white dress. But unlike the latter, she had never aroused any real emotion in me. This astonished me at first, but then I told myself that it was her impeccable beauty, precisely, her very perfection that made it impossible to think of her as a potential "conquest." I probably needed to feel that some little thing about her, at least, was vulnerable, in order to arouse any desire in me to win her.[2]

He later writes: "Her classic features, her cold beauty, her remoteness made me think of some goddess in exile."[3] Here the female characterization is explicit: vulnerability as the main quality of the human; coldness as the main quality of the goddess. As in most fiction, the female characterization is synonymous with an appraisal of the figure's beauty, its type, and most importantly, its effect on the male figures in the book.

Anne, who is, according to Pauline Réage, the other half of Claire, is sweet, modest, vulnerable, young, demure ("Anne, for her part, had resumed the modest demeanor of an object of lust"[4]), and wanton. Claire says that Anne creams at each new humiliation, at even the thought of being whipped. Anne appears to be Beth from *Little Women* but is, in fact, a bitch in heat, her cunt always wet—just like the rest of us, we are meant to conclude. (Beth, remember, died young of goodness.)

Jean de Berg, representing the male sex, is — wouldn't you know it — intelligent, self-assured, quietly master-

ful and self-contained when not actually in the act of
ravaging, powerful and overwhelmingly virile when in
the act of ravaging. One has no idea of his physicality,
except to imagine that he is graying at the temples.

The relationships between the three characters are
structured simply and a bit repetitively: Claire, master—
Anne, slave; Jean de Berg, master—Anne, slave; which
resolves into the happy ending—Jean de Berg, master—
Claire, slave. The master-slave motif is content, structure, and moral of the story. The master role is always
a male role, the slave role is always a female role. The
moral of the story is that Claire, by virtue of her gender,
can only find happiness in the female/slave role.

Here we are told what society would have us know
about lesbian relationships: a man is required for com-
pletion, consummation. Claire is miscast as master because of her literal sex, her genitalia. Jean de Berg is
her surrogate cock which she later forges into the instrument of her own degradation. *The Image* paints
women as real female eunuchs, mutilated in the first
instance, much as Freud suggested, by their lack of
cock, incapable of achieving whole, organic, satisfying
sexual union without the intrusion and participation
of a male figure. That figure cannot only act out the
male role—that figure must possess biological cock and
balls. Claire and Anne as biological females enact a
comedy, grotesque in its slapstick caricature: Claire
as master, a freak by virtue of the role she wills to play,
a role designed to suit the needs and capacities of a
man; Claire as master, as comic as Chaplin doing the
king of France, or Laurel and Hardy falling over each
other's feet in another vain attempt to secure wealth

and success. After all, *The Image* forces us to conclude, what can Claire stick up Anne's cunt but her fingers — hardly instruments of ravishment and ecstasy. Biology, we are told, is role. Biology, we are told, is fate. The message is strangely familiar.

Pauline Réage, the major promoter of *The Image* as a piece of metaphysical veracity, sees the function, or very existence, of the man-master, as the glorification of the woman-slave. Her thesis is that to be a slave is to have power:

> . . . the all powerful slave, dragging herself along the ground at her master's heels, is now really the god. The man is only her priest, living in fear and trembling of her displeasure. His sole function is to perform the various ceremonies that center around the sacred object.[5]

With the logic indigenous to our dual-role culture, the slave is here transmuted into the source of power. What price power, one asks in despair. *This is truly the source of the male notion of female power — since she is at the center of his obsession, she is powerful;* no matter that the form her power takes is that she "drag herself along the ground at her master's heels."

The man, Réage instructs us, has the *illusion* of power because he wields the whip. That illusion marks for Réage the distance between carnal knowledge and what is, more profoundly, true:

> Yes, men are foolish to expect us to revere them when, in the end, they amount to almost nothing. Woman, like man himself, can only worship at the shrine of

that abused body, now loved and now reviled, subjected to every humiliation, but which is, after all,
her own. The man, in this particular affair, stays in one
piece: he is the true worshiper, aspiring in vain to
become one with his god.

The woman, on the contrary, although just as much
of a true worshiper and possessed of that same anxious
regard (for herself) is also the divine object, violated,
endlessly sacrificed yet always reborn, whose only joy,
achieved through a subtle interplay of images, lies in
contemplation of herself.[6]

Having noted in the last chapter Réage's extraordinary
facility with the double-double think, which she uses
here with her usual skill, I must take exception to her
conclusions. It is surprising that the worship of the
divine object, the woman as victim and executioner,
should involve *any* external mediation, especially that
of a male priest. Surely if woman is so willing to be the
giver and the offering, if as "the divine object, violated,
endlessly sacrificed yet always reborn" her "only joy . . .
lies in contemplation of herself," a man is extraneous.
Surely, with such divine endowments and attendant
satisfactions, she need not be coaxed or seduced into
whipping or mutilating herself ("And yet it is usually the
men who introduce their mistresses to the joys of being
chained and whipped, tortured and humiliated . . . ."[7]),
or initiating other women, who serve as a substitute or
mirror image or other half. Men often insist that women
are self-serving, and indeed, Claire is Anne's priestess.
Both execute their roles effectively. No male figure is
required mythologically unless Jean de Berg would play
the eunuch-priest, that traditional helpmate of the

priestess, an honor no doubt not intended for him here. Conversely, only men have been permitted to serve male gods; eunuchs and women, synonymous here, have been strictly excluded from those holy rites. The proper conclusion therefore is that man, not woman, is the divine object of *The Image:* he is the priest; he serves a male god in whose image he was created; he serves himself. Were that not the case, woman, as the worshiped, would serve herself, instead of serving herself up like turkey or duck, garnished, stuffed, sharpened knife ready for the ritual carving. That a man becomes the master of the master means, despite Réage's assertions to the contrary, that women should serve men, that women are properly slaves and men properly masters, that men have the only meaningful power (in our culture—that power allied to and defined by force and violence), that men created in the image of the Almighty are all mighty. Single-single think brings us closer to the truth in this instance than double-double think.

The Image is rife with Christian symbolism. One of the more memorable sequences in the book takes place in a rose garden chosen by Claire as the proper proscenium for Anne's humiliation. In the rose garden, Claire directs Jean de Berg's attention to a specific type of rose, special in its perfect beauty. Claire orders Anne to step into the flowerbed and to fondle the rose, which Anne handles as though it were a moist, ready cunt. Claire orders Anne to pick the rose and to bring it to her, which Anne does, though not before she feebly protests that there is a prohibition against picking the flowers and that she is afraid of the thorns. Anne's hesitation necessitates punishment. She is ordered to lift her dress while Claire first strokes Anne's cunt with the rose, then jabs the thorn into her thigh and tears the flesh very deliberately. Claire kisses Anne's hands as a poetic drop of blood flows. Claire then pushes the stem of the rose into Anne's garter belt. The thorn is caught in the lace, and the flower is fastened, an adornment fraught with symbolic meaning. Even Jean de Berg finds the performance a bit overdone:

> I answered that it was indeed a great success, although perhaps rather overburdened with symbols, in the romantic and surrealist traditions.[8]

The rose as a symbol has powerful occult origins. Eliphas Levi says of it:

> It was the flesh in rebellion against the oppression of spirit; it was Nature testifying that, like grace, she was a daughter of God; it was love refusing to be stifled by the celibate; it was life in revolt against sterility; it was humanity aspiring towards natural religion, full of reason and love, founded on the revelations of the harmony of being, of which the rose, for initiates, was the living floral symbol.[9]

The rose became for Christian mystics "a rose of light in the center of which a human figure is extending its arms in the form of a cross."[10] However, the official Church, in its unending struggle against carnality and nature, posited the rose as a symbol of both in opposition to the lily, which represented purity of mind and body. *The Image* takes a stand on the side of official Christianity by using the rose as an instrument of pain and blood-letting.

The photographs which Claire shows to Jean de Berg are also overflowing with symbolic importance. The photographs are a series of conventional sado-masochistic poses. They chart the torture and mutilation of a victim, in this case Anne, and culminate in what is apparently the brutal stabbing, the actual death, of the victim. Together they reveal a woman's preoccupation with her own body, a narcissism which is concretized in the last photograph, which is of Claire herself, faceless, caressing her own cunt. This narcissism is a flaw which defines woman, and to atone for it a woman must, in the glorious tradition of O, consent to and participate in her own annihilation. Such is the scenario which permits her a Christian salvation, which redeems her of the sin of Eve and the subsequent sin of her own self-love. The photographs are "really nothing more than religious pictures, steps along the way of a new road to the cross." [11] The road, however, is an old one, well traveled, and if the cross is difficult to reach via this particular road, it is only because the bodies of martyrs other than Anne and Claire lie piled so deep.

It is only too obvious that the tortured, mutilated woman who appears first as Anne, then as the more impersonal victim of the photographs, and finally in a dream of Jean de Berg's as a dead body "pierced by many triangular stab wounds in the most propitious areas" [12] is the secular Christ of cunt and breast, Eve's fallen, lustful, carnal descendant, the victim who, unlike Jesus, is suffering for her own sins, the criminal whose punishment scarcely equals the horror of her crime. That crime, of course, is biological womanhood. Jesus died for us once, the crucifixion he suffered sufficed, we are told, for all time. Anne, Claire, O, all will be forced spread-eagle on the cross until death releases them, and then again. No cruelty will ever be proper atonement for their crime, and thus set the rest of us free.

Christianity has one other image of woman, Mary, the Madonna, the Virgin Mother. Jean de Berg dreams of Claire as the Madonna shortly before he beats and fucks her. Surely that demonstrates the psychic significance, in a sexist culture, of the Madonna figure. Just as Anne on the cross was a profanation of the sacred nature of women, so is the concept, the Lie, of a virgin mother, separate from her cunt, separate from nature, innocent by virtue of the abandonment of her real, and most honorable, sexuality.

The worship of virginity must be posited as a real sexual perversion, crueler and more insidious than those sex models condemned by the culture as perverse. The Christian institutionalization of that worship, its cultivation and refinement, have aborted women in the development and expression of natural sexuality by giving credence to that other: woman as whore. The dualism of good and evil, virgin and whore, lily and rose, spirit and nature is inherent in Christianity and finds its logical expression in the rituals of sadomasochism. The Christian emphasis on pain and suffering as the path to transcendence and salvation is the very meat of most sadomasochistic pornography, just as the Christian definition of woman is its justification. Lenny Bruce expressed it very simply when he said this:

> I understand that intellectually—that a woman who sleeps with a different guy every week is a better

Christian than the virgin. Because she has the capacity
to kiss and hug fifty guys a year. And that's what that
act is—kissing and hugging. You can't do it to anyone
you're mad at. If you're just a bit bugged with them,
you can't make it.

So that chick who's got that much love for all her
fellowmen that she can make it with fifty guys a year—
that's intellectually; but emotionally, I don't want to
be the fifty-first guy. Cause I learned my lesson early,
man. The people told me, "This is the way it is, Virgin
is Good, Virgin is Good." Yeah, that's really weird.[13]

As the most obvious male Christ figure of our time, he
should know.

CHAPTER 5

Woman as Victim:
Suck

We move from the straight literary pornography of our forebears, represented by *Story of O* and *The Image*, into another realm, that of the sex newspaper, born of the hip culture (or, as we like to think, counter-culture), post sex revolution (Freudian, Reichian, Mailerian, Brucean, Ginsbergian), post pot, post acid, post pill: post Them and into the world of Us. We move into the realm of here and now, our own turned-on, liberated time and space, into the social world for which we are responsible. Since we seek in that world freedom as women, defined in radical terms, achieved through a concretely lived lifestyle, newspapers like *Suck*, *Oz*, and *Screw* are important. *Playboy* is Them—no doubt Kissinger and Sinatra sleep with it tucked under the pillow. But the counter-culture sex papers are created by people who inhabit our world (freaks, drug users, radicals, longhairs, whatever the appropriate term might be), people who share our values, our concerns—people who talk of liberation. The counter-culture sex papers would be a part of our community and so we are obliged, if we are a community, to approach them critically and seriously, to ask what they bring to us and what they take from us.

"Us"—who are we? Jerry Rubin says that we are the
Children of Amerika. Eldridge Cleaver calls us the
Children of BLOOD. It is our parents, Amerika,
BLOOD, who through their moral bankruptcy and
genocidal ways have forced us from the womb onto the
streets of the nation. It is our parents, Amerika,
BLOOD, whom we refuse to be, whose work we refuse
to do. We are the survivors of Flower Power, now adult,
with our own children. We are the tribes of Woodstock
Nation, now in Diaspora, roaming the whole earth. We
are the New Left, wounded, in disarray. We are not
yet extinct, and we are not nearly finished. Our past
is only prologue.

Generally we are between 24 and 35 years old; have
used acid, mescaline, psilocibin, etc., with some frequency; use grass and hashish often with no mystifica-
tion; have probably used cocaine, amphetamines, or
barbiturates at some time; have frequent sexual relations, many of which are absolutely casual; reject the
nuclear family and seek forms of community antagonistic to it. We are the people who listened to Leary,
Ginsberg, Bruce. Politically we are radicals. Some of
us seek to develop radical forms of community, to live
good, simple, natural lives. Some of us engage in explicitly political actions—opposing illegitimate wars,
resisting the uses of illegitimate authority—we wonder
how to kill pigs without becoming pigs, we are im-
mersed in the *process* of revolution, we learn the skills
of revolution, we resist all forms of current authority
and we simultaneously seek to develop alternatives to
those forms. There are diminishing numbers of peace
freaks among us (totally committed to nonviolent revo-

lution) and quite a few roaring anarchists. We are, at least in our Amerikan manifestation, white, children of privilege, children of liberals and reformists. We were brought up in pretty, clean homes, had lots of privacy, friends, companionship from family and peers. We are unbelievably well educated—we went to fine suburban schools (mostly public) where we experienced physical and intellectual regimentation which we found unbearable; we went to the best colleges and universities (mostly private) where we studied anthropology, Freud, Marx, Norman O. Brown, and Marcuse too, with the finest minds who, it turned out, were chicken shit when it came to applying egalitarian principles in the classroom or outside of it. The universities where we studied all of these disembodied ideas continued doing defense work for the Amerikan government. We have had our share of disaster and despair: the acid tragedies, the Weatherman tragedies, the needle tragedies. Many of us have known jail, and we have all seen friends die. We are older than we ever thought we would be.

What it comes down to is this: through the use of drugs, through sexual living out, through radical political action, we broke through the bourgeois mental sets which were our inheritance but retained the humanism crucial to the liberalism of our parents. Our goals are simple enough to understand: we want to humanize the planet, to break down the national structures which separate us as people, the corporate structures which separate us into distinct classes, the racist structures which separate us according to skin color; to conserve air, water, life in its many forms; to create communities which are more than habitable — communities in which people are free, in which people have what they need, in which groups of people do not accumulate power, or money, or goods, through the exploitation of other people. So when we look at a sex newspaper, made by people like us, we demand that it take some positive step in the direction we want to go: we demand that it incorporate our radical attitudes, the knowledge that acid and other parts of our lifestyle have given us. And, most importantly, we refuse to permit it to reinforce the dual-role sexist patterns and consciousness of this culture, the very patterns and consciousness which oppress us as women, which enslave us as human beings.

Suck is a typical counter-culture sex paper. Any analysis of it reveals that the sexism is all-pervasive, expressed primarily as sadomasochism, absolutely the same as, and not counter to, the parent cultural values. *Suck* claims to be an ally. It is crucial to demonstrate that it is not.

The first issue of *Suck* appeared in Amsterdam, Holland, in 1969. It continues to be printed in Amsterdam because Dutch police do not confiscate pornography or imprison pornographers. It was started by two Amerikan expatriates. *Suck* is entirely about sex, that is, its pages contain pornographic fiction, technical sexual advice (how to suck cock or cunt, for instance), letters from readers which reveal personal sexual histories (mostly celebrational), and photographs of cunt, cock, fucking, sucking, and group orgying. The newspaper appears irregularly — when there is enough money and material for publication. *Suck* is confiscated in England and France with some vigor.

Suck has made positive contributions. Sucking is approached in a new way. Sucking cock, sucking cunt, how to, how good. Sperm tastes good, so does cunt. In particular, the emphasis on sucking cunt serves to demystify cunt in a spectacular way — cunt is not dirty, not terrifying, not smelly and foul; it is a source of pleasure, a beautiful part of female physiology, to be seen, touched, tasted.

The taboo against sucking goes very deep. Most of the actual laws against cocksucking and cuntsucking relate to prohibitions against any sexual activity that does not lead to, or is not performed for the purpose of effecting, impregnation. Sucking as an act leading to orgasm places the nature of sexual contact clearly — sex is the coming together of people for pleasure. The value is in the coming together. Marriage does not sanctify that coming together, procreation is not its goal. *Suck* treats sucking as an act of the same magnitude as fucking. That attitude, pictures of women sucking cock, men sucking cunt, and all the vice versas, discussions of the techniques of sucking, all break down barriers to the realization of a full sexuality.

Cunnilingus and fellatio (sucking by any other name . . .) are still crimes. The antifellatio laws, in conjunction with sodomy laws, are sometimes used against male homosexuals (lesbians are not taken seriously enough to be prosecuted). Given the selective enforcement of the laws, the shame that attaches to the forbidden acts, and the fact that acts of oral lovemaking represented

in words or in pictures are generally deemed obscene,
sucking must be seen in and of itself as an act of political
significance (which is certainly wonderful news for de-
pressed revolutionaries). In this instance *Suck* takes a
relevant, respectable stand.

(Important digression. As late as October 1961,
Lenny Bruce was arrested because in one of his routines
he used the verb "to come" and talked about cocksucking. He was arrested for the *crime* of obscenity.
Bruce described the bust:

> I was arrested for obscenity in San Francisco for using
> a ten letter word which is sort of chic. I'm not going to
> repeat the word tonite. It starts with a "c." They said
> it was vernacular for a favorite homosexual practice —
> which is weird, cause I don't relate that word to homo-
> sexuals. It relates to any contemporary woman I know
> or would know or would love or would marry.[1]

Bruce was busted in San Francisco (obscenity), Philadelphia (possession), Los Angeles (possession), Holly-
wood (obscenity), Chicago (obscenity), and not permitted to enter England or Australia. As late as 1964
Bruce was busted for obscenity in New York City, in
1965 he was declared a legally bankrupt pauper, and
on August 3, 1966, he died in Los Angeles.)

Suck also makes a contribution in printing pictures
of cunt, though here the praise must be severely quali-
fied. Photos of cunt are rare. All the rest we have seen —
siliconed tits, leering smiles, *Playboy*'s version of pubic
hair. But having seen a remarkable movie by Anne
Severson and Shelby Kennedy [2] in which a fixed camera
catalogues the cunts of many different women, all ages,

races, with all sorts of sexual experience, one gets a comprehension of the superficiality of the *Suck* cunt photos. Imagine a catalogue of still photos of people's faces—the colors, textures, indentations, the unique character of each. It is the same with cunts, and it would be fine if *Suck* would show us that. It does not.

Germaine Greer once wrote for *Suck*—she was an editor—and her articles, the token women's articles, were sometimes strong; her voice was always authentic. Her attempt was to bring women into closer touch with unaltered female sexuality and place that sexuality clearly, unapologetically, within the realm of humanity: women, not as objects, but as human beings, truly a revolutionary concept.

But Greer has another side which allies itself with the worst of male chauvinism and it is that side which, I believe, made her articles acceptable to *Suck*'s editors and *Suck* acceptable to her. In an interview in the Amerikan *Screw*, reprinted in *Suck* under the title "Germaine: 'I am a Whore,'" she stated:

> Ideally, you've got to the stage where you really could ball everyone—the fat, the blind, the foolish, the impotent, the dishonest.
> We have to rescue people who are already dead. We have to make love to people who are dead, and that's not easy.[3]

Here is the ever popular notion that women, extending our role as sex object, can humanize an atrophied world. The notion is based on a false premise. Just as the pill was supposed to liberate women by liberating us sexually, i.e., we could fuck as freely as men, fucking is supposed to liberate women and men too. But the pill served to reinforce our essential bondage — it made us more accessible, more open to exploitation. It did not change our basic condition because it did nothing to challenge the sexist structure of society, not to mention conventional sexual relationships and couplings. Neither does promiscuity per se. Greer's alliance with the sexual revolution is, sadly but implicitly, an alliance with male chauvinism because it does not speak to the basic condition of women which remains the same if we fuck one man a week, or twenty.

There is similar misunderstanding in this statement:

> Well, listen, this is one of the things a woman has to understand, and I get a bit impatient sometimes with women who can't see it. A woman, after all, in this country is a commodity. She's a status symbol, and the prettier she is the more expensive, the more difficult to attain. Anyone can have a fat old lady. But young girls with clear eyes are not for the 40-year-old man who's been working as a packer or a storeman all his life. So that when he sees her he snarls, mostly I think, because she's not available to him. She's another taunt, and yet another index of how the American dream is not his to have. He never had a girl like that and he never will.
>
> Now, I think that the most sensible way for us to see the crime of rape is an act of aggression against this property symbol . . . (but I'm not sure about this at all — I mean, I think it's also aggression against the mother who fucks up so many people's lives). And I must think that as a woman, who has not done a revolution, have not put myself on the barricade on this question, I owe it to my poor brothers not to get uptight. Because I am that, I am a woman they could

never hope to ball, and in the back of my mind I reject them too.[4]

Here again, the alliance is with male chauvinism, and it is incomprehensible. Mothers fuck up people's lives in direct proportion to how fucked up their own lives are — that fuck up is the role they must play, the creative possibilities they must abort. Greer surely knows that and must speak to it. Women who walk, as opposed to those who take taxis or drive (another relevant class distinction), are constantly harassed, often threatened with violence, often violated. That is the situation which is the daily life of women.

It is true, and very much to the point, that women are objects, commodities, some deemed more expensive than others — but it is only by asserting one's humanness every time, in all situations, that one becomes someone as opposed to something. That, after all, is the core of our struggle.

Rape, of course, does have its apologists. Norman Mailer posits it, along with murder, as the content of heroism. It is, he tells us in *The Presidential Papers*, morally superior to masturbation. Eldridge Cleaver tells us that it is an act of political rebellion — he "practiced" on Black women so that he could rape white women better. Greer joins the mystifying chorus when she posits rape as an act of aggression against property (a political anticapitalist action no less) and suggests that it might also be an act of psychological rebellion against the ominous, and omnipresent, mother.* Rape

---

* Greer changed her ideas on rape. Cf. Germaine Greer, "Seduction Is a Four-Letter Word," *Playboy*, vol. 20, no. 1 (January 1973).

is, in fact, simple straightforward heterosexual behavior in a male-dominated society. It offends us when it does, which is rarely, only because it is male-female relation without sham—without the mystifying romance of the couple, without the civility of a money exchange. It happens in the home as well as on the streets. It is not a function of capitalism—it is a function of sexism.

What Greer contributes to *Suck,* and to its women readers who might look to her for cogent analysis and deep imagination, is mostly confusion. That confusion stems from an identification with men which too often blunts her perception of the real, empirical problems women face in a sexist society. That confusion manifests itself most destructively in the patently untrue notion that a woman who fucks freely is free.

The main body of *Suck* is pornographic fiction. It is in the fiction that we find a repetition of events, situations, images, and attitudes which most effectively reinforce conventional sexist values. "Congo Crystal Hotel," a story by Mel Clay, is typical of *Suck* fiction. Two men watch a pornographic movie. They have a sadistic sexual encounter. One of the men, Beno, goes off to meet Carol, a woman he has known previously. He forces her to fuck and suck two Blacks, who violate her in every way. Carol's husband intrudes. Beno forces Carol to suck her husband's cock and as her husband comes, Beno shoots him. An example of the purple prose:

> In a sudden spasm the man clutches her head and arches his back and as the beginning sensations of orgasm overtake him Beno pulls the trigger, the explosion drowning out the sound of Carol gulping on his come and his brains splashing against the ceiling.[5]

Carol is announced: "he could smell her even before he saw her." [6] The rape which Beno forces on her is, of course, the vehicle of her recognition that she loves him, because only he could do that to her. The story contains incredible violence. Beno whips his male lover, Carol is beaten and raped, the husband is killed. The cocks of the Blacks are, of course, gigantic tools of pleasure and pain. There is little to distinguish "Congo Crystal Hotel" from straight pornography, except for the awful quality of the writing. The vision of woman is precisely the same: insatiable cunt, to be violated and abused; the sadomasochistic content is the same; even the exaggerated genitalia of the Blacks participate in the worst of the pornographic tradition.

"Sex Angels," a story by Ron Reid, chronicles the adventures of Helen and Tony, that is, a gangbang arranged by Helen with a bunch of tough bikers. Helen is "high class cunt who was soon to be stuffed with their working class cocks." [7] The class analysis is central to the story: "the social gulf accentuated the mounting thrill already high with the knowledge that the young husband was to observe his wife's gangbanging by the pack." [8] The culmination of the event, after Helen has been thoroughly used, is described like this:

> now hot wet fuck tube — hot slit. go on let see you fuck your wife now. we've all been through her. [9]

Helen, whose resemblance to that other well-known sex object, Helen of Troy, will not be overlooked by the acute observer, is a "hot wet fuck tube — hot slit." Indeed, one must ask, in the world of *Suck* fiction, who of us is not?

The overwhelming fact which emerges about *Suck* fiction is that it contains and expresses the traditional male fantasies about women. Helen and Carol differ little from O and Claire. Their needs can be articulated in precisely the same way: cock, lots of it, all of it, all of the time, rape, violation, cruelty. If only our needs were so simple. If only our needs had anything to do with it at all.

Men have always known, in that existential-according-to-Mailer way, that women not only need IT but want IT, rape-brand-whip orchestrated. It was always obvious to them — a woman's "virtue" is merely façade, her reluctance is merely tactic. What matters is that she wants to be fucked — she is defined by her need to be fucked. We find in *Suck* these sacrosanct male fantasies applied with true counter-culture egalitarianism: to all beings "feminine," whether women or gay men. Projection has come home to roost and cock is crowing like never before — but, like the cult of cunt before it, the cult of cock is colored with the washes of unresolved guilt and pure sadism. The onus and hatred of male homosexuality is heavy in *Suck* — ugly, heavy, and ever present.

Suck has in some ways aligned itself with the cause of gay liberation. *Suck 4* printed the "Gay Guide to Europe," a list of gay clubs, bars, pissoirs, etc., to alleviate the chronic need for information felt by the traveling gay man. *Suck 6* has a story entitled "A Week in the Fondle Park," in which a man extols the quantity of cock sucked in one idyllic week in Amsterdam's central park, which had been turned over to long-haired dopers and freaks in the summer of 1971. But in *Suck,* as in the parent culture which maligns any

deviation from the ole hetero norm, the hatred attached
to the queer is very apparent.

"The Suction Game" is the story of two men, one
dark-skinned, one light-skinned, one overt, one latent —
a typical colonial situation, ripe for exploitation. The
acknowledged (overt) queer has the typical misogynist
point of view:

> Carlos explained that the male body was nature's
> perfection and how clean men were compared to
> women.[10]

To the normal(ly) self-enhancing John Wayne male, the
above is self-evident and always has been. In the context of the homosexual encounter it has added significance. It reinforces the maleness of both partners. It
makes the homosexual act an affirmation of manhood.
The insecurities which a homosexual identity conjures
up in our culture, however, are hardly resolved through
the putting down of women. "Cocksucker" is a term of
insult and abuse — it means queer. Yet it is obviously
absurd for a man to believe that what is pleasurable to
him when done by a woman is disgusting when done by
a man. The distinction here is not so very subtle: the
political meaning of the two acts, heterosexual fellatio
and homosexual fellatio, is different. The former makes
the man clearly the master — the woman kneels at the
foot of the sheikh. The latter makes the man *queer* —
ours is not to reason why, or is it?

Carlos (overt, dark-skinned), having unzipped the
hero's pants, has started kissing his glorious equip-
ment:

> Here I was standing in this tiny YMCA room, naked as
> the day I was born, with a pretty boy queer, kneeling
> in front of me playing with my cock. The whole thing
> was sickening, but the worst part was that I was en-
> joying it. . . . Suddenly I didn't give a fuck if he was
> queer. I just relaxed and surrendered to his sucking
> mouth.[11]

The resultant orgasm is fantastic, mind-blowing, as
aren't they all in *Suck*. Yet the imminent slander is too
much to bear. Being sucked by a queer is one thing.
Reciprocity is something else. Could it be reciprocity
that makes one queer?

> He was a fucking queer but I wasn't. If he had hot
> rock that was his problem not mine. He'll just have to
> find some other queer to suck his cock.[12]

Hot Rock Carlos is undaunted. After much patient
persistance, our supermale hero succumbs, with res-
ervations: "The idea was repulsive to me, but I wanted
to make him happy." [13] The moral of the tale is simple.
Says our hero:

> Funny I do not consider myself queer, just damn lucky
> to be able to attract so many good looking young boys
> so they could have their rock inside me.[14]

Only now does the definitive definition of queer seem
to emerge. Cocksucking isn't the definitive experience
after all. One must conclude that anal intercourse,
the closest corollary to female penetration, really defines the queer. One must conclude that being fucked
in the ass separates the queers from the men and places

them squarely among the women. One must conclude that being penetrated is queer, not to mention debasing, disgusting, and humiliating, which one had already guessed.

Homosexual men are not only penetrated like women — they also lust after pain and degradation. The author of "The Suction Game" has given us another example of homosexual pornography, this one engagingly entitled "Tough Young Dicks for Hot Kicks." Five young toughs are cruising; they pick up a long-haired boy, shove him in the back seat of the car and order him to blow them all; the boy considers refusing, since he'd love to be beaten then and there, but instead submits since greater abuse can always be had through submission than through resistance; the young toughs brutally rape the long-haired boy, then piss and shit all over him. He is, of course, ecstatic:

> Gee did I smell of come and teenage sweat and urine and I had two more toss-offs myself thinking about their tough young faces and dicks enjoying me for hot kicks.[15]

The stereotype of the homosexual which emerges from the general run of *Suck* fiction is not very different from the stereotype of woman. The homosexual is queer, asshole, cocksucker, faggot; the woman is hole, hot wet fuck tube, hot slit, or just plain ass. He thrives on pain and so does she. Gangbanging is their mutual joy. Huge, throbbing, monster, atom-smashing cock is god and master to them both. The parts they play in the sadomasochistic script are the same: so are costumes, attitudes, and other conventional cultural baggage. It

is not hard to see that the struggle for gay male liberation and women's liberation is a common struggle:
both mean freedom from the stigma of being female.
The fantasies (indicative of structural mental sets) which
oppress male homosexuals and women are very much
alike. Women and male homosexuals are united in
their queerness, a union which is real and verifiable —
affirmed by *Suck*, which contributes to the cultural
oppression of both.

The pages of *Suck* have, sadly, nothing to do with
sexual liberation — there is no "counter" to the culture to be found anywhere in them. They are, instead,
a catalogue of exactly those sexist fantasies which
express our most morbid psychic sets. They chart the
landscape of repression, a landscape that is surprisingly
familiar. As women, we find that we are where we have
always been: the necessary victim, there we are, the
victim again; the eternal object, there we are, the object again. Through the projection of archetypal sadomasochistic images, which are the staple of the sexist
mentality, we become more a prisoner, robbed and
cheated of any real experience or authentic communication, thrown back into the intricate confusion of being
women in search of a usable identity.

Part Three

THE HERSTORY

We are a feelingless people. If we could really feel, the pain would be so great that we would stop all the suffering. If we could feel that one person every six seconds dies of starvation (and as this is happening, this writing, this reading, someone is dying of starvation) we would stop it. If we could really feel it in the bowels, the groin, in the throat, in the breast, we would go into the streets and stop the war, stop slavery, stop the prisons, stop the killings, stop destruction. Ah, I might learn what love is.

When we feel, we will feel the emergency: when we feel the emergency, we will act: when we act, we will change the world.

Julian Beck, *The Life of the Theatre*

The rapes, tortures, and violations of O, Claire, Anne, *Suck*'s Helen, et al., are fiction, documenting the twisted landscape of male wish-fulfillment. Here we have herstory, the underbelly of history, two acts of gynocide committed against women by men, their scope and substance largely ignored. One is not surprised to find that they document that same twisted landscape.

I isolate in particular Chinese footbinding and the persecution of the witches because they are crimes which equal in sheer horror and sadism the extermination of Native Americans and Hitler's massacre of the Jews. Those two horrendous slaughters have found a place, however tenuous, in the "conscience" of "man." Acts of genocide against women have barely been noticed, and they have never evoked rage, or horror, or sorrow. That sexist hatred equals racist hatred in its intensity, irrationality, and contempt for the sanctity of human life these two examples clearly demonstrate. That women have not been exterminated, and will not be (at least until the technology of creating life in the laboratory is perfected) can be attributed to our presumed ability to bear children and, more importantly no doubt, to the relative truth that men prefer to fuck cunts who are nominally alive. I except here necrophiliacs, those pure and unsullied princes, whose story begins where ours ends.

In addition, in any war, in any violence between tribes or nations, a specific war crime is perpetrated against women—that of rape. Every woman raped during a political nation-state war is the victim of a much larger war, planetary in its dimensions—the war, more declared than we can bear to know, that men wage against women. That war had its most gruesome, grotesque expression when Chinese men bound the feet of Chinese women and when British, Welsh, Irish, Scottish, German, Dutch, French, Swiss, Italian, Spanish, and Amerikan men had women burned at the stake in the name of God the Father and His only Son.

Instructions Before Reading Chapter

1. Find a piece of cloth 10 feet long and 2 inches wide
2. Find a pair of children's shoes
3. Bend all toes except the big one under and into the sole of the foot. Wrap the cloth around these toes and then around the heel. Bring the heel and toes as close together as possible. Wrap the full length of the cloth as tightly as possible
4. Squeeze foot into children's shoes
5. Walk
6. Imagine that you are 5 years old
7. Imagine being like this for the rest of your life

CHAPTER 6

Gynocide: Chinese Footbinding

The origins of Chinese footbinding, as of Chinese thought in general, belong to that amorphous entity called antiquity. The 10th century marks the beginning of the physical, intellectual, and spiritual dehumanization of women in China through the institution of footbinding. That institution itself, the implicit belief in its necessity and beauty, and the rigor with which it was practiced lasted another 10 centuries. There were sporadic attempts at emancipating the foot—some artists, intellectuals, and women in positions of power were the proverbial drop in the bucket. Those attempts, modest though they were, were doomed to failure:

footbinding was a political institution which reflected and perpetuated the sociological and psychological inferiority of women; footbinding cemented women to a certain sphere, with a certain function — women were sexual objects and breeders. Footbinding was mass attitude, mass culture — it was the key reality in a way of life lived by real women — 10 centuries times that many millions of them.

It is generally thought that footbinding originated as an innovation among the dancers of the Imperial harem. Sometime between the 9th and 11th centuries, Emperor Li Yu ordered a favorite ballerina to achieve the "pointed look." The fairy tale reads like this:

> Li Yu had a favored palace concubine named Lovely Maiden who was a slender-waisted beauty and a gifted dancer. He had a six-foot high lotus constructed for her out of gold; it was decorated lavishly with pearls and had a carmine lotus carpet in the center. Lovely Maiden was ordered to bind her feet with white silk cloth to make the tips look like the points of a moon sickle. She then danced in the center of the lotus, whirling about like a rising cloud.[1]

From this original event, the bound foot received the euphemism "Golden Lotus," though it is clear that Lovely Maiden's feet were bound loosely — she could still dance.

A later essayist, a true foot gourmand, described 58 varieties of the human lotus, each one graded on a 9-point scale. For example:

TYPE: Lotus petal, New moon, Harmonious bow, Bamboo shoot, Water chestnut
SPECIFICATIONS: plumpness, softness, fineness

RANK:

  Divine Quality (A-1), perfectly plump, soft and fine
  Wondrous Quality (A-2), weak and slender
  Immortal Quality (A-3), straight-boned, independent
  Precious Article (B-1), peacocklike, too wide, disproportioned
  Pure Article (B-2), gooselike, too long and thin
  Seductive Article (B-3), fleshy, short, wide, round (the disadvantage of this foot was that its owner *could* withstand a blowing wind)
  Excessive Article (C-1), narrow but insufficiently pointed
  Ordinary Article (C-2), plump and common
  False Article (C-3), monkeylike large heel (could climb)

The distinctions only emphasize that footbinding was a rather hazardous operation. To break the bones involved or to modify the pressure of the bindings irregularly had embarrassing consequences—no girl could bear the ridicule involved in being called a "large-footed Demon" and the shame of being unable to marry.

Even the possessor of an A-1 Golden Lotus could not rest on her laurels—she had to observe scrupulously the taboo-ridden etiquette of bound femininity: (1) do not walk with toes pointed upwards; (2) do not stand with heels seemingly suspended in midair; (3) do not move skirt when sitting; (4) do not move feet when lying down. The same essayist concludes his treatise with this most sensible advice (directed to the gentlemen of course):

Do not remove the bindings to look at her bare feet, but be satisfied with its external appearance. Enjoy the outward impression, for if you remove the shoes and bindings the aesthetic feeling will be destroyed forever.[2]

Indeed. The real feet looked like this:

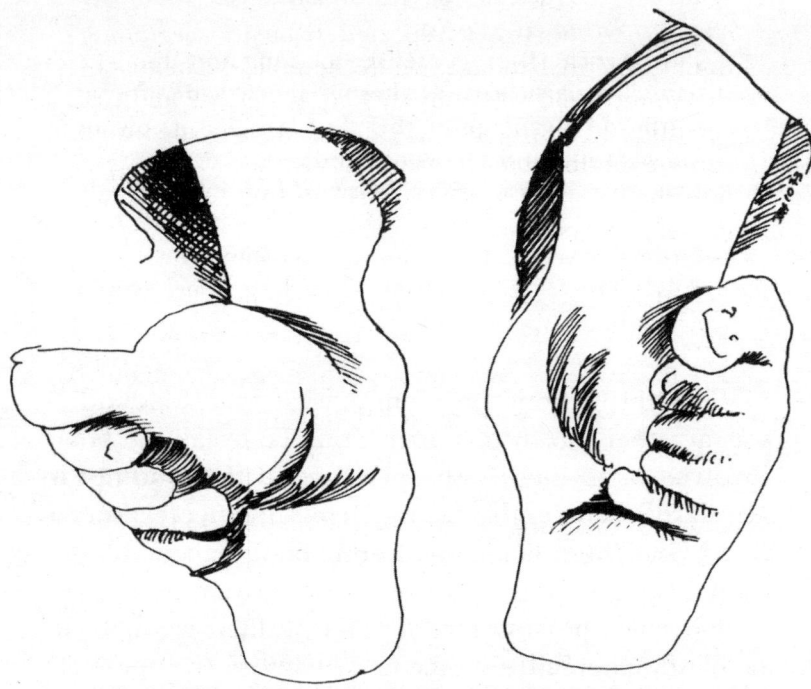

(*feet: 3 to 4 inches in length*)

The physical process which created this foot is described by Howard S. Levy in *Chinese Footbinding: The History of a Curious Erotic Custom:*

The success or failure of footbinding depended on skillful application of a bandage around each foot. The bandage, about two inches wide and ten feet long, was wrapped in the following way. One end was placed on the inside of the instep, and from there it was carried over the small toes so as to force the toes in and towards the sole. The large toe was left unbound. The bandage was then wrapped around the heel so forcefully that heel and toes were drawn closer together. The process was then repeated from the beginning until the entire bandage had been applied. The foot of the young child was subjected to a coercive and unremitting pressure, for the object was not merely to confine the foot but to make the toes bend under and into the sole and bring the heel and sole as close together as physically possible.[3]

A Christian missionary observed:

The flesh often became putrescent during the binding and portions sloughed off from the sole; sometimes one or more toes dropped off.[4]

An elderly Chinese woman, as late as 1934, remembered vividly her childhood experience:

Born into an old-fashioned family at P'ing-hsi, I was inflicted with the pain of footbinding when I was seven years old. I was an active child who liked to jump about, but from then on my free and optimistic nature vanished. Elder Sister endured the process from six to eight years of age [this means that it took Elder Sister two years to attain the 3-inch foot]. It was in the first lunar month of my seventh year that my ears were pierced and fitted with gold earrings. I was told that a girl had to suffer twice, through ear piercing and footbinding. Binding started in the second lunar month; mother consulted references in order to select an auspicious day for it. I wept and hid in a neighbor's home, but Mother found me, scolded me, and dragged me home. She shut the bedroom door, boiled water, and from a box withdrew binding, shoes, knife, needle, and thread. I begged for a one-day postponement, but Mother refused: "Today is a lucky day," she said. "If bound today, your feet will never hurt; if bound tomorrow they will." She washed and placed alum on my feet and cut the toenails. She then bent my toes toward the plantar with a binding cloth ten feet long and two inches wide, doing the right foot first and then the left. She finished binding and ordered me to walk, but when I did the pain proved unbearable.

That night, Mother wouldn't let me remove the shoes. My feet felt on fire and I couldn't sleep; Mother struck me for crying. On the following days, I tried to hide but was forced to walk on my feet. Mother hit me on my hands and feet for resisting. Beatings and curses were my lot for covertly loosening the wrappings. The feet were washed and rebound after three or four days, with alum added. After several months, all toes but the big one were pressed against the inner surface. Whenever I ate fish or freshly killed meat, my feet would swell, and the pus would drip. Mother criticized me for placing pressure on the heel in walking, saying that my feet would never assume a pretty shape. Mother would remove the bindings and wipe the blood and pus which dripped from my feet. She told me that only with the removal of the flesh could my feet become slender. If I mistakenly punctured a sore, the blood gushed like a stream. My somewhat fleshy big toes were bound with small pieces of cloth and forced upwards, to assume a new moon shape.

Every two weeks, I changed to new shoes. Each new pair was one- to two-tenths of an inch smaller than the previous one. The shoes were unyielding, and it took pressure to get into them. Though I wanted to sit passively by the K'ang, Mother forced me to move around. After changing more than ten pairs of shoes, my feet were reduced to a little over four inches. I had been in binding for a month when my younger sister started; when no one was around, we would weep together. In summer, my feet smelled offensively because of pus and blood; in winter, my feet felt cold because of lack of circulation and hurt if they got too near the K'ang and were struck by warm air currents. Four of the toes were curled in like so many dead caterpillars; no outsider would ever have believed that they belonged to a human being. It took two years to achieve the three-inch model. My toenails pressed against the flesh like thin paper. The heavily-creased plantar couldn't be scratched when it itched or soothed when it ached. My shanks were thin, my feet became humped, ugly, and odiferous; how I envied the natural-footed! [5]

Bound feet were crippled and excruciatingly painful. The woman was actually "walking" on the outside of toes which had been bent under into the sole of the foot. The heel and instep of the foot resembled the sole and heel of a high-heeled boot. Hard callouses formed; toenails grew into the skin; the feet were pus-filled and bloody; circulation was virtually stopped. The footbound woman hobbled along, leaning on a cane, against a wall, against a servant. To keep her balance she took very short steps. She was actually falling with every step and catching herself with the next. Walking required tremendous exertion.

Footbinding also distorted the natural lines of the female body. It caused the thighs and buttocks, which were always in a state of tension, to become somewhat swollen (which men called "voluptuous"). A cu-

rious belief developed among Chinese men that footbinding produced a most useful alteration of the
vagina. A Chinese diplomat explained:

> The smaller the woman's foot, the more wondrous
> become the folds of the vagina. (There was the say-
> ing: the smaller the feet, the more intense the sex
> urge.) Therefore marriages in Ta-t'ung (where binding
> is most effective) often take place earlier than else-
> where. Women in other districts can produce these
> folds artificially, but the only way is by footbinding,
> which concentrates development in this one place.
> There consequently develop layer after layer (of folds
> within the vagina); those who have personally ex-
> perienced this (in sexual intercourse) feel a super-
> natural exaltation. So the system of footbinding was
> not really oppressive.[6]

Medical authorities confirm that physiologically footbinding had no effect whatsoever on the vagina, although it did distort the direction of the pelvis. The
belief in the wondrous folds of the vagina of footbound
woman was pure mass delusion, a projection of lust
onto the feet, buttocks, and vagina of the crippled
female. Needless to say, the diplomat's rationale for
finding footbinding "not really oppressive" confused
his "supernatural exaltation" with her misery and
mutilation.

Bound feet, the same myth continues, "made the
buttocks more sensual, [and] concentrated life-giving
vapors on the upper part of the body, making the face
more attractive."[7] If, due to a breakdown in the flow
of these "life-giving vapors," an ugly woman was footbound and still ugly, she need not despair, for an A-1

Golden Lotus could compensate for a C-3 face and figure.

But to return to herstory, how did our Chinese ballerina become the millions of women stretched over 10 centuries? The transition from palace dancer to population at large can be seen as part of a class dynamic. The emperor sets the style, the nobility copies it, and the lower classes climbing ever upward do their best to emulate it. The upper class bound the feet of their ladies with the utmost severity. The Lady, unable to walk, remained properly invisible in her boudoir, an ornament, weak and small, a testimony to the wealth and privilege of the man who could afford to keep her — to keep her idle. Doing no manual labor, she did not need her feet either. Only on the rarest of occasions was she allowed outside of the incarcerating walls of her home, and then only in a sedan chair behind heavy curtains. The lower a woman's class, the less could such idleness be supported: the larger the feet. The women who had to work for the economic survival of the family still had bound feet, but the bindings were looser, the feet bigger — after all, she had to be able to walk, even if slowly and with little balance.

Footbinding was a visible brand. *Footbinding did not emphasize the differences between men and women — it created them*, and they were then perpetuated in the name of morality. Footbinding functioned as the Cerberus of morality and ensured female chastity in a nation of women who literally could not "run around." Fidelity, and the legitimacy of children, could be reckoned on.

The minds of footbound women were as contracted

as their feet. Daughters were taught to cook, supervise
the household, and embroider shoes for the Golden
Lotus. Intellectual and physical restriction had the usual
male justification. Women were perverse and sinful,
lewd and lascivious, if left to develop naturally. The
Chinese believed that being born a woman was payment
for evils committed in a previous life. Footbinding was
designed to spare a woman the disaster of another such
incarnation.

Marriage and the family are the twin pillars of all
patriarchal cultures. Bound feet, in China, were the
twin pillars of these twin pillars. Here we have the joining together of politics and morality, coupled to produce their inevitable offspring—the oppression of
women based on totalitarian standards of beauty and a
rampant sexual fascism. In arranging a marriage, a
male's parents inquired first about the prospective
bride's feet, then about her face. Those were her human, recognizable qualities. During the process of footbinding, mothers consoled their daughters by conjur-
ing up the luscious marriage possibilities dependent on
the beauty of the bound foot. Concubines for the Imperial harem were selected at tiny-foot festivals (forerunners of Miss America pageants). Rows upon rows
of women sat on benches with their feet outstretched
while audience and judges went along the aisles and
commented on the size, shape, and decoration of foot
and shoes. No one, however, was ever allowed to touch
the merchandise. Women looked forward to these
festivals, since they were allowed out of the house.

The sexual aesthetics, literally the art of love, of

the bound foot was complex. The sexual attraction of the foot was based on its concealment and the mystery surrounding its development and care. The bindings were unwrapped and the feet were washed in the woman's boudoir, in the strictest privacy. The frequency of bathing varied from once a week to once a year. Perfumes of various fragrances and alum were used during and after washing, and various kinds of surgery were performed on the callouses and nails. The physical process of washing helped restore circulation. The mummy was unwrapped, touched up, and put back to sleep with more preservatives added. The rest of the body was never washed at the same time as the feet, for fear that one would become a pig in the next life. Well-bred women were supposed to die of shame if men observed them washing their feet. The foot consisted, after all, of smelly, rotted flesh. This was naturally not pleasing to the intruding male, a violation of his aesthetic sensibility.

The art of the shoes was basic to the sexual aesthetics of the bound foot. Untold hours, days, months went into the embroidery of shoes. There were shoes for all occasions, shoes of different colors, shoes to hobble in, shoes to go to bed in, shoes for special occasions like birthdays, marriages, funerals, shoes which denoted age. Red was the favored color for bed shoes because it accentuated the whiteness of the skin of the calves and thighs. A marriageable daughter made about 12 pairs of shoes as a part of her dowry. She presented 2 specially made pairs to her mother-in-law and father-in-law. When she entered her husband's home for the first time, her feet were immediately examined by the whole family, neither praise nor sarcasm being withheld.

There was also the art of the gait, the art of sitting, the art of standing, the art of lying down, the art of adjusting the skirt, the art of every movement which involves feet. Beauty was the way feet looked and how they moved. Certain feet were better than other feet, more beautiful. Perfect 3-inch form and utter uselessness were the distinguishing marks of the aristocratic foot. These concepts of beauty and status defined women: as ornaments, as sexual playthings, as sexual constructs. The perfect construct, even in China, was naturally the prostitute.

The natural-footed woman generated horror and repulsion in China. She was anathema, and all the forces of insult and contempt were used to obliterate her. Men said about bound feet and natural feet:

> A tiny foot is proof of feminine goodness. . . .
> Women who don't bind their feet, look like men, for the tiny foot serves to show the differentiation. . . .
> The tiny foot is soft and, when rubbed, leads to great excitement. . . .
> The graceful walk gives the beholder mixed feelings of compassion and pity. . . .
> Natural feet are heavy and ponderous as they get into bed, but tiny feet lightly steal under the coverlets. . . .
> The large-footed woman is careless about adornment, but the tiny-footed frequently wash and apply a variety of perfumed fragrances, enchanting all who come into their presence. . . .

The natural foot looks much less aesthetic in walking. . . .

Everyone welcomes the tiny foot, regarding its smallness as precious. . . .

Men formerly so craved it that its possessor achieved harmonious matrimony. . . .

Because of its diminutiveness, it gives rise to a variety of sensual pleasures and love feelings. . . .[8]

Thin, small, curved, soft, fragrant, weak, easily inflamed, passive to the point of being almost inanimate—this was footbound woman. Her bindings created extraordinary vaginal folds; isolation in the bedroom increased her sexual desire; playing with the shriveled, crippled foot increased everyone's desire. Even the imagery of the names of various types of foot suggest, on the one hand, feminine passivity (lotuses, lilies, bamboo shoots, water chestnuts) and, on the other hand, male independence, strength, and mobility (lotus boats, large-footed crows, monkey foot). It was unacceptable for a woman to have those male qualities denoted by large feet. This fact conjures up an earlier assertion: footbinding did not formalize existing differences between men and women—it created them. One sex became male by virtue of having made the other sex some thing, something other, something completely polar to itself, something called female. In 1915, a satirical essay in defense of footbinding, written by a Chinese male, emphasized this:

The bound foot is the condition of a life of dignity for man, of contentment for woman. Let me make this clear. I am a Chinese fairly typical of my class. I pored

too much over classic texts in my youth and dimmed
my eyes, narrowed my chest, crooked my back. My
memory is not strong, and in an old civilization there
is a vast deal to learn before you can know anything.
Accordingly among scholars I cut a poor figure. I am
timid, and my voice plays me false in gatherings of
men. But to my footbound wife, confined for life to
her house except when I bear her in my arms to her
palanquin, my stride is heroic, my voice is that of a
roaring lion, my wisdom is of the sages. To her I am
the world; I am life itself.[9]

Chinese men, it is clear, stood tall and strong on
women's tiny feet.

The so-called art of footbinding was the process of
taking the human foot, using it as though it were in-
sensible matter, molding it into an inhuman form. Footbinding was the "art" of making living matter insensi-
ble, inanimate. We are obviously not dealing here with
art at all, but with fetishism, with sexual psychosis. This
fetish became the primary content of sexual experience
for an entire culture for 1,000 years. The manipulation
of the tiny foot was an indispensable prelude to all
sexual experience. Manuals were written elaborating
various techniques for holding and rubbing the Golden
Lotus. Smelling the feet, chewing them, licking them,
sucking them, all were sexually charged experiences.
A woman with tiny feet was supposedly more easily
maneuvered around in bed and this was no small ad-
vantage. Theft of shoes was commonplace. Women
were forced to sew their shoes directly onto their bindings. Stolen shoes might be returned soaked in semen.
Prostitutes would show their naked feet for a high

price (there weren't many streetwalkers in China). Drinking games using cups placed in the shoes of prostitutes or courtesans were favorite pastimes. Tiny-footed prostitutes took special names like Moon Immortal, Red Treasure, Golden Pearl. No less numerous were the euphemisms for feet, shoes, and bindings. Some men went to prostitutes to wash the tiny foot and eat its dirt, or to drink tea made from the washing water. Others wanted their penises manipulated by the feet. Superstition also had its place — there was a belief in the curative powers of the water in which tiny feet were washed.

Lastly, footbinding was the soil in which sadism could grow and go unchecked — in which simple cruelty could transcend itself, without much effort, into atrocity. These are some typical horror stories of those times:

> A stepmother or aunt in binding the child's foot was usually much harsher than the natural mother would have been. An old man was described who delighted in seeing his daughters weep as the binding was tightly applied. . . . In one household, everyone had to bind. The main wife and concubines bound to the smallest degree, once morning and evening, and once before retiring. The husband and first wife strictly carried out foot inspections and whipped those guilty of having let the binding become loose. The sleeping shoes were so painfully small that the women had to ask the master to rub them in order to bring relief. Another rich man would flog his concubines on their tiny feet, one after another, until the blood flowed.[10]

. . . about 1931 . . . bound-foot women unable to flee
had been taken captive. The bandits, angered because
of their captives' weak way of walking and inability to
keep in file, forced the women to remove the bindings
and socks and run about barefoot. They cried out in
pain and were unable to move on in spite of beatings.
Each of the bandits grabbed a woman and forced her
to dance about on a wide field covered with sharp
rocks. The harshest treatment was meted out to prostitutes. Nails were driven through their hands and
feet; they cried aloud for several days before expiring.
One form of torture was to tie-up a woman so that her
legs dangled in midair and place bricks around each
toe, increasing the weight until the toes straightened
out and eventually dropped off.[11]

END OF FOOTBINDING EVENT

One asks the same questions again and again, over
a period of years, in the course of a lifetime. The questions have to do with people and what they do—the how
and the why of it. How could the Germans have mur-
dered 6,000,000 Jews, used their skins for lampshades,
taken the gold out of their teeth? How could white
people have bought and sold black people, hanged
them and castrated them? How could "Americans"
have slaughtered the Indian nations, stolen the land,
spread famine and disease? How can the Indochina
genocide continue, day after day, year after year?
How is it possible? Why does it happen?

As a woman, one is forced to ask another series of
hard questions: Why everywhere the oppression of
women throughout recorded history? How could the

Inquisitors torture and burn women as witches? How could men idealize the bound feet of crippled women? How and why?

The bound foot existed for 1,000 years. In what terms, using what measure, could one calculate the enormity of the crime, the dimensions of the transgression, the *amount* of cruelty and pain inherent in that 1,000-year herstory? In what terms, using what vocabulary, could one penetrate to the meaning, to the reality, of that 1,000-year herstory?

Here one race did not war with another to acquire food, or land, or civil power; one nation did not fight with another in the interest of survival, real or imagined; one group of people in a fever pitch of hysteria did not destroy another. None of the traditional explanations or justifications for brutality between or among peoples applies to this situation. On the contrary, here one sex mutilated (enslaved) the other in the interest of the *art* of sex, male-female *harmony,* role-definition, beauty.

Consider the magnitude of the crime.

Millions of women, over a period of 1,000 years, were brutally crippled, mutilated, in the name of erotica.

Millions of human beings, over a period of 1,000 years, were brutally crippled, mutilated, in the name of beauty.

Millions of men, over a period of 1,000 years, reveled in love-making devoted to the worship of the bound foot.

Millions of men, over a period of 1,000 years, worshiped and adored the bound foot.

Millions of mothers, over a period of 1,000 years, brutally crippled and mutilated their daughters for the sake of a secure marriage.

Millions of mothers, over a period of 1,000 years, brutally crippled and mutilated their daughters in the name of beauty.

But this thousand-year period is only the tip of an awesome, fearful iceberg: an extreme and visible expression of romantic attitudes, processes, and values organically rooted in all cultures, then and now. It demonstrates that man's love for woman, his sexual adoration of her, his human definition of her, his delight and pleasure in her, require her negation: physical crippling and psychological lobotomy. That is the very nature of romantic love, which is the love based on polar role definitions, manifest in herstory as well as in fiction—he glories in her agony, he adores her deformity, he annihilates her freedom, he will have her as sex object, even if he must destroy the bones in her feet to do it. Brutality, sadism, and oppression emerge as the substantive core of the romantic ethos. That ethos is the warp and woof of culture as we know it.

Women should be beautiful. All repositories of cultural wisdom from King Solomon to King Hefner agree: women should be beautiful. It is the reverence for female beauty which informs the romantic ethos, gives it its energy and justification. Beauty is transformed into that golden ideal, Beauty—rapturous and abstract. Women must be beautiful and Woman is Beauty.

Notions of beauty always incorporate the whole of a

given societal structure, are crystallizations of its values. A society with a well-defined aristocracy will have aristocratic standards of beauty. In Western "democracy" notions of beauty are "democratic": even if a woman is not born beautiful, she can make herself *attractive*.

The argument is not simply that some women are not beautiful, therefore it is not fair to judge women on the basis of physical beauty; or that men are not judged on that basis, therefore women also should not be judged on that basis; or that men should look for character in women; or that our standards of beauty are too parochial in and of themselves; or even that judging women according to their conformity to a standard of beauty serves to make them into products, chattels, differing from the farmer's favorite cow only in terms of literal form. The issue at stake is different, and crucial. Standards of beauty describe in precise terms the relationship that an individual will have to her own body. They prescribe her mobility, spontaneity, posture, gait, the uses to which she can put her body. *They define precisely the dimensions of her physical freedom.* And, of course, the relationship between physical freedom and psychological development, intellectual possibility, and creative potential is an umbilical one.

In our culture, not one part of a woman's body is left untouched, unaltered. No feature or extremity is spared the art, or pain, of improvement. Hair is dyed, lacquered, straightened, permanented; eyebrows are plucked, penciled, dyed; eyes are lined, mascaraed, shadowed; lashes are curled, or false—from head to toe, every feature of a woman's face, every section of her body, is subject to modification, alteration. This alteration is an ongoing, repetitive process. It is vital to the economy, the major substance of male-female role differentiation, the most immediate physical and psychological reality of being a woman. From the age of 11 or 12 until she dies, a woman will spend a large part of her time, money, and energy on binding, plucking, painting, and deodorizing herself. It is commonly and wrongly said that male transvestites through the use of makeup and costuming caricature the women they would become, but any real knowledge of the romantic ethos makes clear that these men have penetrated to the core experience of being a woman, a romanticized construct.

The technology of beauty, and the message it carries, is handed down from mother to daughter. Mother teaches daughter to apply lipstick, to shave under her arms, to bind her breasts, to wear a girdle and high-heeled shoes. Mother teaches daughter concomitantly her role, her appropriate behavior, her place. Mother teaches daughter, necessarily, the psychology which defines womanhood: a woman must be beautiful, in order to please the amorphous and amorous Him. What we have called the romantic ethos operates as vividly in 20th-century Amerika and Europe as it did in 10th-century China.

This cultural transfer of technology, role, and psychology virtually affects the emotive relationship between mother and daughter. It contributes substantially to the ambivalent love-hate dynamic of that relationship. What must the Chinese daughter/child have felt toward the mother who bound her feet? What does any daughter/child feel toward the mother who forces her to do painful things to her own body? The mother takes on the role of enforcer: she uses seduction, command, all manner of force to coerce the daughter to conform to the demands of the culture. It is because this role becomes her dominant role in the mother-daughter relationship that tensions and difficulties between mothers and daughters are so often unresolvable. The daughter who rejects the cultural norms enforced by the mother is forced to a basic rejection of her own mother, a recognition of the hatred and resentment she felt toward that mother, an alienation from mother and society so extreme that her own womanhood is denied by both. The daughter who internalizes those values and endorses those same processes is bound to repeat the teaching she was taught—her anger and resentment remain subterranean, channeled against her own female offspring as well as her mother.

Pain is an essential part of the grooming process, and that is not accidental. Plucking the eyebrows, shaving under the arms, wearing a girdle, learning to walk in high-heeled shoes, having one's nose fixed, straightening or curling one's hair—these things *hurt*. The pain, of course, teaches an important lesson: no price is too great, no process too repulsive, no operation too painful for the woman who would be beautiful. *The tolerance of pain and the romanticization of that tolerance begins here,* in preadolescence, in socialization, and serves to prepare women for lives of childbearing, self-abnegation, and husband-pleasing. The adolescent experience of the "pain of being a woman" casts the feminine psyche into a masochistic mold and forces the adolescent to conform to a self-image which bases itself on mutilation of the body, pain happily suffered, and restricted physical mobility. It creates the masochistic personalities generally found in adult women: subservient, materialistic (since all value is placed on the body and its ornamentation), intellectually restricted, creatively impoverished. It forces women to be a sex of lesser accomplishment, weaker, as underdeveloped as any backward nation. Indeed, the effects of that prescribed relationship between women and their bodies are so extreme, so deep, so extensive, that scarcely any area of human possibility is left untouched by it.

Men, of course, like a woman who "takes care of herself." The male response to the woman who is made-up and bound is a learned fetish, societal in its dimensions. One need only refer to the male idealization of the bound foot and say that the same dynamic is operating here. Romance based on role differentiation, superiority based on a culturally determined and rigidly enforced inferiority, shame and guilt and fear of women and sex itself: all necessitate the perpetuation of these oppressive grooming imperatives.

The meaning of this analysis of the romantic ethos surely is clear. A first step in the process of liberation (women from their oppression, men from the unfreedom of their fetishism) is the radical redefining of the relationship between women and their bodies. The body must be freed, liberated, quite literally: from paint and girdles and all varieties of crap. Women must stop mutilating their bodies and start living in them. Perhaps the notion of beauty which will then organically emerge will be truly democratic and demonstrate a respect for human life in its infinite, and most honorable, variety.

BEAUTY HURTS

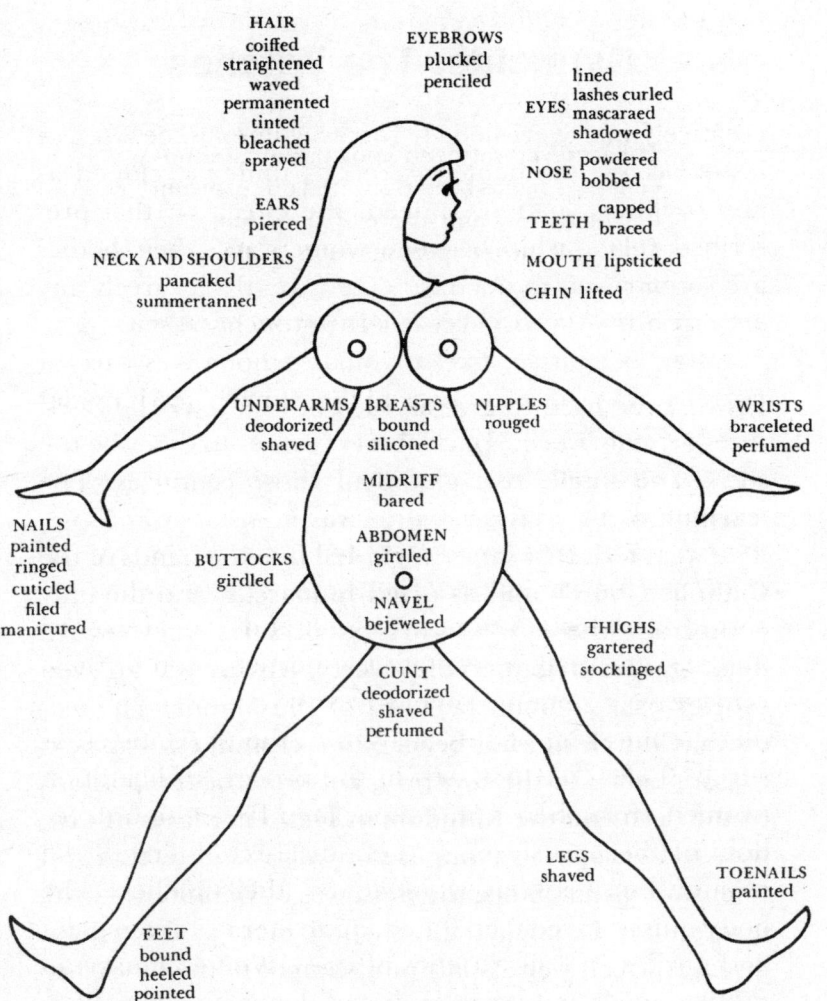

HAIR
coiffed
straightened
waved
permanented
tinted
bleached
sprayed

EYEBROWS
plucked
penciled

EYES
lined
lashes curled
mascaraed
shadowed

NOSE
powdered
bobbed

EARS
pierced

TEETH
capped
braced

NECK AND SHOULDERS
pancaked
summertanned

MOUTH lipsticked

CHIN lifted

UNDERARMS
deodorized
shaved

BREASTS
bound
siliconed

NIPPLES
rouged

WRISTS
braceleted
perfumed

MIDRIFF
bared

NAILS
painted
ringed
cuticled
filed
manicured

ABDOMEN
girdled

BUTTOCKS
girdled

NAVEL
bejeweled

THIGHS
gartered
stockinged

CUNT
deodorized
shaved
perfumed

LEGS
shaved

TOENAILS
painted

FEET
bound
heeled
pointed

RIDDLE

Q: Why haven't women made great works of art?

A: Because they are great works of art.

CHAPTER 7

Gynocide: The Witches

It has never yet been known that an innocent person has been punished on suspicion
of witchcraft, and there is no doubt that
God will never permit such a thing to
happen.

Malleus Maleficarum

It would be hard to give an idea of how dark the Dark
Ages actually were. "Dark" barely serves to describe the
social and intellectual gloom of those centuries. The
learning of the classical world was in a state of eclipse.
The wealth of that same world fell into the hands of the
Catholic Church and assorted monarchs, and the only
democracy the landless masses of serfs knew was a
democratic distribution of poverty. Disease was an even
crueler exacter than the Lord of the Manor. The medieval Church did not believe that cleanliness was next
to godliness. On the contrary, between the temptations
of the flesh and the Kingdom of Heaven, a layer of dirt,
lice, and vermin was supposed to afford protection and
to ensure virtue. Since the flesh was by definition sinful,
it was not to be uncovered, washed, or treated for those
diseases which were God's punishment in the first place
—hence the Church's hostility to the practice of medicine and to the search for medical knowledge. Abetted
by this medieval predilection for filth and shame, successive epidemics of leprosy, epileptic convulsions,

and plague decimated the population of Europe regularly. The Black Death is thought to have killed 25 percent of the entire population of Europe; two-thirds to one-half of the population of France died; in some towns every living person died; in London it is estimated that one person in ten survived:

> On Sundays, after Mass, the sick came in scores, crying for help and words were all they got: You have sinned, and God is afflicting you. Thank Him: you will suffer so much the less torment in the life to come. Endure, suffer, die. Has not the Church its prayers for the dead.[1]

Hunger and misery, the serf's constant companions, may well have induced the kinds of hallucinations and hysteria which profound ignorance translated as demonic possession. Disease, social chaos, peasant insurrections, outbreaks of dancing mania (tarantism) with its accompanying mass flagellation—the Church had to explain these obvious evils. What kind of Shepherd was this whose flock was so cruelly and regularly set upon? Surely the hell-fires and eternal damnation which were vivid in the Christian imagination were modeled on daily experience, on real earth-lived life.

The Christian notion of the nature of the Devil underwent as many transformations as the snake has skins. In this evolution, natural selection played a determining role as the Church bred into its conception those deities best suited to its particular brand of dualistic theology. It is a cultural constant that the gods of one religion become the devils of the next, and the Church, intolerant of deviation in this as in all other areas, vilified the gods of those pagan religions which threatened Catholic supremacy in Europe until at least the 15th century. The pagan religions were not monotheistic and their pantheons were scarcely conservative in number. The Church had a slew of deities to dispatch and would have done so speedily had not the old gods their faithful adherents who clung to the old practices, who had local power, who had to be pacified. Accordingly, the Church did a kind of roulette and sent some gods to heaven (canonizing them) and others to hell (damning them). Especially in southern Europe the local deities, formerly housed on Olympus, were allowed to continue their traditional vocations of healing the sick and protecting the traveler. The Church often transformed the names of the gods — so as not to be embarrassed, no doubt. Apollo, for instance, became St. Apollinaris; Cupid became St. Valentine. The pagan gods were also allowed to retain their favorite haunts — shrines, trees, wells, burial grounds, now newly decorated with a cross.

But in northern Europe the old gods did not fare as well. The peoples of northern Europe were temperamentally and culturally quite different from the Latin Christians, and their religions centered around animal totemism and fertility rites. The "heathens" adhered to a primitive animism. They worshiped nature (archenemy of the Church), which was manifest in spirits who inhabited stones, rivers, and trees. In the paleolithic hunting stage, they were concerned with magical control of animals. In the later neolithic agricultural stage, fertility practices to ensure the food supply predominated.

Anthropologists now believe that man's first representation of any anthropomorphic deity is that of a horned figure who wears a stag's head and is apparently dancing. That figure is to be found in a cavern in Arriège. Early religions actively worshiped animals, and in particular animals which symbolized male fertility—the bull, goat, or stag. Ecstatic dancing, feasts, sacrifice of the god or his representative (human or animal) were parts of the rites. The magician-priest-shaman became the earthly incarnation of the god-animal and apparently dressed in the skins of the sacred animal (even the Pharaoh of Egypt had an animal tail attached to his girdle). There he stood, replete with horns and hooves—the primitive deity, attributes of him echoing in the later deities Osiris, Isis, Hathor, Pan, and Janus. His worship was assimilated into the phallic worship of the northern sky-thunder-warrior gods (the influence of which can be seen in Druidic practices). These pagan rites and deities maintained their divinity in the mass psyche despite all of the Church's attempts to blacklist them. Some kings of England were converted by the missionaries, only to revert to the old faith when the missionaries left. Others maintained two altars, one devoted to Christ, one to the horned god. The peasants never played politics—they clung to the fertility-magic beliefs. Until the 10th century, the Church protested this willful "devil worship" but could do nothing but issue proclamations, impose penances and fasts, and, of course, carry on the unending struggle against nature and the flesh.

This was a serious business, for the end of the world was believed to be imminent. For good Christians, prep-

arations to depart this earthly abode included renunciation of all hedonistic activities (eating, dancing, fucking, etc.). St. Simon Stylites, in his attempt to avoid the
crime of being human, fled to the desert where he
erected a pillar on which he mortified his flesh for most
of his 72 years. He was tempted throughout by visions
of lascivious women. Indeed, it required starvation,
incessant prayer, and flagellation to be visited by lascivious women in those days and still lead the perfect
Christian life.

The extremeness of the Church's ascetic imperatives
invited a reciprocal debauchery. The nobility, when
not out butchering, enforced that most curious of
customs, the *jus primae noctis,* which legitimated the rape
of newly wed peasant women. The Crusaders brought
back spices and syphilis from the East—that summing
up their knowledge of Arab culture. The clergy was
so openly corrupt and sensual that successive popes
were forced to acknowledge it. "By 1102 a church coun-
cil had to state specifically that priests should be degraded for sodomy and anathematized for 'obstinate
sodomy.'" [2] Bishops and cardinals were also known to
fuck around: "A typical example is that Bishop of Toul
... whose favorite concubine was his own daughter
by a nun of Epinal." [3] The monasteries and cloisters
were rampant with homosexuality, but nuns and monks
did occasionally get together for heterosexual fucking.

Until the 12th century, there were basically three
kinds of relationship to the Church. There were the
ascetics who fled the cities to roam like beasts in the
wilderness and emulated St. Simon, who made a pig-sty
his home when not on the pillar. The ascetics mortified

the flesh while awaiting cataclysmic destruction and eternal resurrection. There were the nobility, the clergy, and the soldiers, who delighted in carnal excesses of every sort, and the serfs who went on breeding because it was their only outlet and because the nobles encouraged increases in the number of tenants. The last group, crucial to this period, were the heretics. In the 12th century various groups, viewing the abominations of Christianity with increasing horror, began to voice openly and even loudly their skepticism. These sects played a prominent role in shaping the Church's idea of the Devil.

The Waldenses, Manicheans, and Cathari were the principal heretical sects. It is said that "the Waldenses were burnt for the practices for which the Franciscans were later canonized."[4] Their crime was to expose and to mock the clergy as frauds. For their piety they suffered the fate of all heretics, which was burning. More influential and more dangerous were the Manicheans, who traced their origins to the Persian Mani who had been crucified in A.D. 276. The Manicheans worshiped one God, who incorporated both good and evil, the ancient Zoroastrian idea. The Cathari, who were equally maligned by the Christians, also worshiped the dual principle:

> . . . the chief outstanding quality of the Cathari was their piety and charity. They were divided into two sections: the ordinary lay believers and the Perfecti, who believed in complete abstinence and even the logical end of all asceticism — the Endura — a passionate disavowal of physical humanity which led them to starvation and even apparently to mass suicide. They

adopted most of the Christian teaching and dogma of
the New Testament, mixed with Gnostic ritual, using
asceticism as an end to visions and other-consciousness.
They were so loyal to their beliefs that a John of Tou-
louse was able to plead before his judges in 1230 . . .
"Lords: hear me. I am no heretic; for I have a wife and
lie with her, and have children; and I eat flesh and lie
and swear, and am a faithful Christian." Many of them
seem, indeed, to have lived with the barren piety of
the saints. They were accordingly accused of sexual
orgies and sacrilege, and burned, and scourged, and
harried. Nevertheless the heresy flourished, and
Cathari were able to hold conferences on equal terms
with orthodox bishops.[5]

The Holy Inquisition, in its infancy, exterminated the
Cathari, tried to exterminate the Jews, and then went
on to exterminate the Knights Templars, the Christian
organization of knighthood and conquest which had
become too powerful and wealthy. It had become independent of clergy and kings, and had thereby in-
curred the wrath of both. With these experiences under
its expanding belt, the Inquisition in the 15th century
turned to the persecution of those most heinous of all
heretics, the witches, that is, to all of those who still clung
to the old cult beliefs of pagan Europe.

The Manicheans and Cathari had, in order to account for the existence of good and evil (the thorniest of
theological problems), worshiped good and evil both.
The Catholics, not able to accept that solution, developed a complex theology concerning the relationship between God and the Devil, now called Satan,
which rested on the weird idea that Satan was limited
in some specific ways, but very marvelous, all of his

machinations, curses, and damnations being "by God's permission" and a testimony to God's divine majesty. Here we have the Catholic version of double-double think. Through the processes of Aristotle's famous logic, as adapted by St. Thomas Aquinas, which was the basis of Catholic theology, it now became clear that not to believe in the literal existence of Satan was tantamount to atheism. The evil principle, articulated by the Manicheans and Cathari, was absorbed into Catholicism, along with the horned figure of the old pagan cults, to produce the horned, clawed, sulphurous, black, fire and brimstone Satan of the medieval Christian iconographers.

Later Calvin and Luther also made their contributions. Luther had more personal contact with Satan than any man before or since. He proclaimed Satan "Prince" of this earthly realm and considered all earthly experiences under his domination. Luther and Calvin agreed that good works no longer counted — only divine grace for the elect was sufficient to ensure entrance into the Kingdom of God. Thus Reformation Protestantism obliterated the small measure of hope that even Catholicism offered. Calvin himself was a voracious witch hunter and burner.

Although the Protestants contributed without modesty and with great enthusiasm to the witch terror, we find the origins of the actual, organized persecutions, not unexpectedly, in the Bull of Innocent VIII, issued December 9, 1484. The Pope named Heinrich Kramer and James Sprenger as Inquisitors and asked them to define witchcraft, describe the *modus operandi* of witches, and standardize trial procedures and sen-

tencing. The papal Bull reversed the Church's previous
position, which had been formulated by a synod in
A.D. 785:

> . . . if somebody, deceived by the devil, following the
> custom of the heathen, believes that some man or
> woman, is a striga who eats men, and for that reason
> burns her or gives her flesh to eat, or eats it, he is to
> be punished by death.[6]

The Church had accordingly for 7 centuries considered
the belief in witchcraft a heathen belief and the burning of alleged witches a capital crime. Pope Innocent,
however, secure in papal infallibility and demonstrat-
ing a true political sensibility (leading to the consolida-
tion of power), described the extent of his concern:

> It has indeed lately come to Our ears, not without
> afflicting Us with bitter sorrow, that in some parts of
> Northern Germany, as well as in the provinces, town-
> ships, territories, districts, and dioceses of Mainz,
> Cologne, Treves, Saltzburg, and Bremen, many
> persons of both sexes, unmindful of their own salva-
> tion and straying from the Catholic Faith, have aban-
> doned themselves to devils, *incubi* [male] and *succubi*
> [female], and by their incantations, spells, conjurations,
> and other accursed charms and crafts, enormities and
> horrid offenses, have slain infants yet in the mother's
> womb, as also the offspring of cattle, have blasted the
> produce of the earth, the grapes of the vine, the fruit
> of the trees, nay, men and women, beasts of burthen,
> herd beasts, as well as animals of other kinds, vine-
> yards, orchards, meadows, pastureland, corn, wheat,
> and all other cereals; these wretches furthermore af-
> flict and torment men and women, beasts of burthen,

herd beasts, as well as animals of other kinds, with
terrible and piteous pains and sore diseases, both internal and external; they hinder men from performing
the sexual act and women from conceiving, whence
husbands cannot know their wives nor wives receive
their husbands; over and above this, they blasphe-
mously renounce that Faith which is theirs by the
Sacrament of Baptism, and at the instigation of the
Enemy of Mankind they do not shrink from commit-
ting and perpetrating the foulest abominations and
filthiest excesses to the deadly peril of their own souls,
whereby they outrage Divine Majesty and are a cause
of scandal and danger to very many.[7]

To deal with the increasing tide of witchcraft and
in conformity with the Pope's orders, Sprenger and
Kramer collaborated on the *Malleus Maleficarum*. This
document, a monument to Aristotle's logic and academic methodology (quoting and footnoting "authorities"), catalogues the major concerns of 15th-century
Catholic theology:

Question I. Whether the Belief that there are such
Beings as Witches is so Essential a Part of the Catholic
Faith that Obstinancy to maintain the Opposite Opinion
manifestly savours of Heresy (Answer: Yes)

Question III. Whether Children can be Generated by
Incubi and Succubi (Answer: Yes)

Question VIII. Whether Witches can Hebetate the Power
of Generation or Obstruct the Venereal Act (Answer:
Yes)

Question IX. Whether Witches may work some Presti-
digitatory Illusion so that the Male Organ appears to

be entirely removed and separate from the Body (Answer: Yes)

Question XI. That Witches who are Midwives in Various Ways Kill the Child Conceived in the Womb, and Procure Abortion; or if they do not do this, Offer New-born Children to the Devils (Answer: Yes) [8]

The *Malleus* also describes the ritual and content of witchcraft per se, though in the tradition of paternalism indigenous to the Church, Sprenger and Kramer are careful not to give formulae for charms or other dangerous information. They write "of the several Methods by which Devils through Witches Entice and Allure the Innocent to the Increase of that Horrid Craft and company"; "of the Way whereby a Formal Pact with Evil is made"; "How they are Transported from Place to Place"; "Here follows the Way whereby Witches copulate with those Devils known as Incubi," [9] etc. They document how witches injure cattle, cause hailstorms and tempests, illnesses in people and animals, bewitch men, change themselves into animals, change animals into people, commit acts of cannibalism and murder. The main concern of the *Malleus* is with natural events, nature, the real dynamic world which refused to conform to Catholic doctrine — the *Malleus,* with tragic wrong-headedness, explains most aspects of biology, sexology, medicine, and weather in terms of the demonic.

Before we approach the place of women in this most Christian piece of Western history, the importance of the *Malleus* itself must be understood. In the Dark Ages, few people read and books were hard to come by. Yet the *Malleus* was printed in numerous editions. It was found in every courtroom. It had been read by every judge, each of whom would know it chapter and verse. The *Malleus* had more currency than the Bible. It was theology, it was law. To disregard it, to challenge its authority ("seemingly inexhaustible wells of wisdom," [10] wrote Montague Summers in *1946*, the year I was born) was to commit heresy, a capital crime.

Although statistical information on the witchcraft persecutions is very incomplete, there are judicial records extant for particular towns and areas which are accurate:

> In almost every province of Germany the persecution raged with increasing intensity. Six hundred were said to have been burned by a single bishop in Bamberg, where the special witch jail was kept fully packed. Nine hundred were destroyed in a single year in the bishopric of Wurzburg, and in Nuremberg and other great cities there were one or two hundred burnings a year. So there were in France and in Switzerland. A thousand people were put to death in one year in the district of Como. Remigius, one of the Inquisitors, who was author of *Daemonolatvia*, and a judge at Nancy boasted of having personally caused the burning of nine hundred persons in the course of fifteen years. Delrio says that five hundred were executed in Geneva in three terrified months in 1515. The Inquisition at Toulouse destroyed four hundred persons in a single execution, and there were fifty at Douai in a single year. In Paris, executions were continuous. In the Pyrenees, a wolf country, the popular form was that of the *loup-garou*, and De L'Ancre at Labout burned two hundred. [11]

It is estimated that at least 1,000 were executed in England, and the Scottish, Welsh, and Irish were even

fiercer in their purges. It is hard to arrive at a figure
for the whole of the Continent and the British Isles,
but the most responsible estimate would seem to be
9 million. It may well, some authorities contend, have
been more. Nine million seems almost moderate when
one realizes that The Blessed Reichhelm of Schongan at
the end of the 13th century computed the number of
the Devil-driven to be 1,758,064,176. A conservative,
Jean Weir, physician to the Duke of Cleves, estimated
the number to be only 7,409,127. The ratio of women to
men executed has been variously estimated at 20 to 1
and 100 to 1. Witchcraft was a woman's crime.

Men were, not surprisingly, most often the bewitched. Subject to women's evil designs, they were terrified victims. Those men who were convicted of witchcraft were often family of convicted women witches, or
were in positions of civil power, or had political ambi-
tions which conflicted with those of the Church, a
monarch, or a local dignitary. Men were protected from
becoming witches not only by virtue of superior intellect and faith, but because Jesus Christ, phallic divinity,
died "to preserve the male sex from so great a crime:
since He was willing to be born and to die for us, therefore He has granted to men this privilege." [12] Christ
died literally for *men* and left women to fend with the
Devil themselves. Without the personal intercession of
Christ, women remained what they had always been in
Judeo-Christian culture:

> Now the wickedness of women is spoken of in
> *Ecclesiasticus* xxv: There is no head above the head
> of a serpent: and there is no wrath above the wrath of

a woman. I had rather dwell with a lion and a dragon than to keep house with a wicked woman. And among much which in that place precedes and follows about a wicked woman, he concludes: All wickedness is but little to the wickedness of a woman. Wherefore S. John Chrysostom says on the text. It is not good to marry (S. Matthew xix): What else is woman but a foe to friendship, an unescapable punishment, a necessary evil, a natural temptation, a desirable calamity, a domestic danger, a delectable detriment, an evil nature, painted with fair colours! . . . Cicero in his second book of *The Rhetorics* says: The many lusts of men lead them into one sin, but the one lust of women leads them into all sins; for the root of all woman's vices is avarice. . . . When a woman thinks alone, she thinks evil.[13]

The word "woman" means "the lust of the flesh. As it is said: I have found a woman more bitter than death, and a good woman subject to carnal lust."[14]

Other characteristics of women made them amenable to sin and to partnership with Satan:

And the first is, that they are more credulous. . . . The second reason is, that women are naturally more impressionable, and more ready to receive the influence of a disembodied spirit. . . .

The third reason is that they have slippery tongues, and are unable to conceal from their fellow-women those things which by evil arts they know; and since they are weak, they find an easy and secret manner of vindicating themselves by witchcraft. . . .

. . . because in these times this perfidy is more often found in women than in men, as we learn by actual experience, if anyone is curious as to the reason, we may add to what has already been said the following:

that since they are feebler both in mind and body, it is not surprising that they should come more under the spell of witchcraft.

For as regards intellect, or the understanding of spiritual things, they seem to be of a different nature from men; a fact which is vouched for by the logic of the authorities, backed by various examples from the Scriptures. Terence says: Women are intellectually like children.[15]

Women are by nature instruments of Satan — they are by nature carnal, a structural defect rooted in the original creation:

> But the natural reason is that she is more carnal than a man, as is clear from her many carnal abominations. And it should be noted that there was a defect in the formation of the first woman, since she was formed from a bent rib, that is, rib of the breast, which is bent as it were in a contrary direction to a man. And since through this defect she is an imperfect animal, she always deceives. . . . And all this is indicated by the etymology of the word; for *Femina* comes from *Fe* and *Minus,* since she is ever weaker to hold and preserve the Faith. And this as regards faith is of her very nature. . . .[16]

> . . . This is so even among holy women, so what must it be among others?[17]

In addition, "Women also have weak memories," "woman will follow her own impulse even to her own destruction," "nearly all the kingdoms of the world have been overthrown by women," "the world now suffers through the malice of women," "a woman is beautiful to look upon, contaminating to the touch, and deadly to keep,"

"she is a liar by nature," "her gait, posture, and habit
. . . is vanity of vanities." [18]

Women are most vividly described as being "more
bitter than death":

> And I have found a woman more bitter than death,
> who is the hunter's snare, and her heart is a net, and
> her hands are bands. He that pleaseth God shall es-
> cape from her; but he that is a sinner shall be caught
> by her. More bitter than death, that is, than the
> devil. . . .
>
> More bitter than death, again, because that is
> natural and destroys only the body; but the sin which
> arose from woman destroys the soul by depriving it
> of grace, and delivers the body up to the punishment
> for sin.
>
> More bitter than death, again, because bodily death
> is an open and terrible enemy, but woman is a wheedling
> and secret enemy. [19]

and also:

> And that she is more perilous than a snare does not
> speak of the snare of hunters, but of devils. For men
> are caught not only through their carnal desires, when
> they see and hear women: for S. Bernard says: Their
> face is a burning wind, and their voice the hissing of
> serpents. . . . And when it is said that her heart is a
> net, it speaks of the inscrutable malice which reigns
> in their hearts. . . .
>
> To conclude: All witchcraft comes from carnal lust,
> which is in women insatiable. See Proverbs xxx: there
> are three things that are never satisfied, yea, a fourth
> thing which says not, it is enough; that is, the mouth
> of the womb. [20]

Here the definition of woman, in common with the
pornographic definition, is her carnality; the essence
of her character, in common with the fairy-tale definition, is her malice and avarice. The words flow almost
too easily in our psychoanalytic age: we are dealing
with an existential terror of women, of the "mouth of
the womb," stemming from a primal anxiety about male
potency, tied to a desire for self (phallic) control; men
have deep-rooted castration fears which are expressed
as a horror of the womb. These terrors form the sub-
strata of a myth of feminine evil which in turn justified
several centuries of gynocide.

The evidence, provided by the *Malleus* and the ex-
ecutions which blackened those centuries, is almost
without limit. One particular concern was that devils
stole semen (vitality) from innocent, sleeping men —
seductive witches visited men in their sleep, and did the
evil stealing. As Ernest Jones wrote:

> The explanation for these fantasies is surely not hard.
> A nightly visit from a beautiful or frightful being who
> first exhausts the sleeper with passionate embraces and
> withdraws from him a vital fluid: all this can point
> only to a natural and common process, namely to
> nocturnal emissions accompanied by dreams of a more
> or less erotic nature. In the unconscious mind blood is
> commonly an equivalent for semen.[21]

To be dreamed of often ended in slow burning on the
stake.

The most blatant proof of the explicitly sexual nature of the persecutions, however, had to do with one of
the witches' most frequent crimes: they cast "glamours".

over the male organ so that it disappeared entirely. Sprenger and Kramer go to great lengths to prove that witches do not actually remove the genital, only render it invisible. If such a glamour lasts for under 3 years, a marriage cannot be annulled; if it lasts for 3 years or longer, it is considered a permanent fact and does annul any marriage. Catholics now seeking grounds for divorce should perhaps consider using that one.

Men lost their genitals quite frequently. Most often, the woman responsible for the loss was a cast-off mistress, maliciously turned to witchcraft. If the bewitched man could identify the woman who had afflicted him, he could demand reinstatement of his genitals:

> A young man who had lost his member and suspected a certain woman, tied a towel about her neck, choked her and demanded to be cured. "The witch touched him with her hand between the thighs, saying, 'Now you have your desire.'" His member was immediately restored.[22]

Often the witches, greedy by virtue of womanhood, were not content with the theft of one genital:

> And what then is to be thought of those witches who in this way sometimes collect male organs, as many as twenty or thirty members together, and put them in a bird's nest or shut them up in a box, where they move themselves like living members and eat oats and corn, as has been seen by many as is a matter of common report?[23]

How can we understand that millions of people for centuries believed as literal truth these seemingly idi-

otic allegations? How can we begin to comprehend that
these beliefs functioned as the basis of a system of ju-
risprudence that condemned 9 million persons, mostly
women, to being burned alive? The literal text of the
Malleus Maleficarum, with its frenzied and psychotic
woman-hating and the fact of the 9 million deaths,
demonstrates the power of the myth of feminine evil,
reveals how it dominated the dynamics of a culture,
shows the absolute primal terror that women, as carnal
beings, hold for men.

We see in the text of the *Malleus* not only the fear of
loss of potency or virility, but of the genitals themselves — a dread of the loss of cock and balls. The reason
for this fear can perhaps be located in the nature of
the sex act per se: men enter the vagina hard, erect;
men emerge drained of vitality, the cock flaccid. The
loss of semen, and the feeling of weakness which is its
biological conjunct, has extraordinary significance to
men. Hindu tradition, for instance, postulates that men
must either expel the semen and then vacuum it back
up into the cock, or not ejaculate at all. For those Western men for whom orgasm is simultaneous with
ejaculation, sex must be a most literal death, with
the mysterious, muscled, pulling vagina the death-
dealer.

To locate the origins of the myth of feminine evil
in male castration and potency fears is not so much to
participate in the Freudian world view as it is to accept
and apply the anthropologist's method and link up
Western Judeo-Christian man with Australian, African,
or Trobriand primitives. To do so is to challenge the
egotism which informs our historical attitude toward

ourselves and which would separate us from the rest of the species. There is nothing to indicate that "civilization," "culture," and/or Christianity have in any way moderated the primal male dread of castration. Quite the contrary, *his*tory might even be defined as the study of the concrete expression of that dread.

The Christians in their manifold variety were continuing the highly developed Jewish tradition of misogyny, patriarchy, and sexist suppression, alternatively known as the Garden-of-Eden-Hype. The Adam and Eve creation myth is *the* basic myth of man and woman, creation, death, and sex. There is another Jewish legend, namely that of Adam-Lilith, which never assumed that place because it implies other, nonsexist, nonpatriarchal values. The Genesis account of Adam and Eve in Eden involves, according to Hays, three themes: "the transition from primitive life to civilization, the coming of death, and the acquisition of knowledge."[24] As Hays points out, Adam has been told by God the Father that if he eats from the Tree of Knowledge he will die. The serpent tells Eve that she and Adam will not die. The serpent, it turns out, told the immediate truth: Adam and Eve do not keel over dead; rather, they know each other carnally.

Sex is, biblically speaking, the sole source of civilization, death, and knowledge. As punishment, Adam must go to work and Eve must bear children. We have here the beginning of the human family and the work ethic, both tied to guilt and sexual repression by virtue of their origins. One could posit, with all the assurance of a Monday-morning quarterback, that Adam and Eve always were mortal and carnal and that through eating the forbidden fruit only became aware of what their condition had always been. God has never been very straightforward with people.

Whether the precise moral of the story is that death is a direct punishment for carnal knowledge (which might make guilt an epistemological corollary) or that awareness of sex and death are coterminous, the fact of man knowing and feeling guilt is rooted in the Oedipal content of the legend. In a patriarchy, one does not disobey the father.

Adam's legacy post-Eden is sexual knowledge, mortality, guilt, toil, and the fear of castration. Adam became a human male, the head of a family. His sin was lesser than Eve's, seemingly by definition again. Even in Paradise, wantonness, infidelity, carnality, lust, greed, intellectual inferiority, and a metaphysical stupidity earmark her character. Yet her sin was greater than Adam's. God had, in his oft-noted wisdom, created her in a way which left her defenseless against the wiles of the snake—the snake approached her for that very reason. Yet she bears responsibility for the fall. Double-double think is clearly biblical in its origins.

Eve's legacy was a twofold curse: "Unto the woman He said: 'I will greatly multiply thy pain and thy travail; in pain thou shalt bring forth children; and thy desire shall be to thy husband, and he shall rule over thee.' " [25] Thus, the menstrual cycle and the traditional agony of childbirth do not comprise the full punishment—patriarchy is the other half of that ancient curse.

The Christians, of course, like Avis, trying harder, seeing in woman the root of all evil, limited her to breeding more sinners for the Church to save. No wonder then that women remained faithful adherents of the older totemic cults of Western Europe which honored female sexuality, deified the sexual organs and reproductive capacity, and recognized woman as embodying the regenerative power of nature. The rituals of these cults, centering as they did on sexual potency, birth, and phenomena connected to fertility, had been developed by women. Magic was the substance of ritual, the content of belief. The magic of the witches was an imposing catalogue of medical skills concerning reproductive and psychological processes, a sophisticated knowledge of telepathy, auto- and hetero-suggestion, hypnotism, and mood-controlling drugs. Women knew the medicinal nature of herbs and developed formulae for using them. The women who were faithful to the pagan cults developed the science of organic medicine, using vegetation, before there was any notion of the *profession* of medicine. Paracelsus, the most famous physician of the Middle Ages, claimed that everything he knew he had learned from "the good women." [26]

Experimenting with herbs, women learned that those which would kill when administered in large doses had curative powers when administered in smaller amounts. Unfortunately, it is as poisoners that the witches are remembered. The witches used drugs like belladonna and aconite, organic amphetamines, and hallucinogenics. They also pioneered the development of analgesics. They performed abortions, provided all medical help for births, were consulted in cases of impotence which they treated with herbs and hypnotism, and were the first practitioners of euthanasia. Since the Church enforced the curse of Eve by refusing to permit

any alleviation of the pain of childbirth, it was left to
the witches to lessen pain and mortality as best they
could. It was especially as midwives that these learned
women offended the Church, for, as Sprenger and
Kramer wrote, "No one does more harm to the Catholic
Faith than midwives." [27] The Catholic objection to abortion centered specifically on the biblical curse which
made childbearing a painful punishment—it did not
have to do with the "right to life" of the unborn fetus.
It was also said that midwives were able to remove labor
pains from the woman and transfer those pains to her
husband—clearly in violation of divine injunction and
intention both.

The origins of the magical content of the pagan cults
can be traced back to the fairies, who were a real, neolithic people, smaller in stature than the natives of
northern Europe or England. They were a pastoral
people who had no knowledge of agriculture. They
fled before stronger, technologically more advanced
murderers and missionaries who had contempt for
their culture. They set up communities in the in-
lands and concealed their dwellings in mounds half
hidden in the ground. The fairies developed those
magical skills for which the witches, centuries later,
were burned.

The socioreligious organization of the fairy culture
was matriarchal and probably polyandrous. The fairy
culture was still extant in England as late as the 17th
century when even the pagan beliefs of the early witches
had degenerated into the Christian parody which we
associate with Satanism. The Christians rightly recognized the fairies as ancient, original sorcerers, but

wrongly saw their whole culture as an expression of the
demonic. There was communication between the fairies
and the pagan women, and any evidence that a woman
had visited the fairies was considered sure proof that
she was a witch.

There were, then, three separate, though interre-
lated, phenomena: the fairy race with its matriarchal
social organization, its knowledge of esoteric magic
and medicine; the woman-oriented fertility cults, also
practitioners of esoteric magic and medicine; and later,
the diluted witchcraft cults, degenerate parodies of
Christianity. There is particular confusion when one
tries to distinguish between the last two phenomena.
Many of the women condemned by the Inquisition were
true devotees of the Old Religion. Many were confused by Christian militancy and aggression, not to
mention torture and threat of burning, and saw themselves as diabolical, damned witches.

An understanding of what the Old Religion really
was, how it functioned, is crucial if we want to understand the precise nature of the witch hunt, the amount
and kind of distortion that the myth of feminine evil
made possible, who the women were who were being
burned, and what they had really done. The information available comes primarily from the confessions
of accused witches, recorded and distorted by the Inquisitors, and from the work of anthropologists like
Margaret Murray and C. L'Estrange Ewen. The scenario of the witchcraft cults is pieced together from
those sources, but many pieces are missing. A lot of
knowledge disappears with 9 million people.

The religion was organized with geographic integ-

rity. Communities had their own organizations, mainly
structured in covens, with local citizens as administra-
tors. There were weekly meetings which took care of
business—they were called esbats. Then there were
larger gatherings, called sabbats, where many covens
met together for totemic festivities. There may have
been an actual continental organization with one all-
powerful head, but evidence on this point is ambiguous.
It was a proselytizing religion in that nonmembers were
approached by local officials and asked to join. Conditions of membership in a coven were the free consent
of the individual, abjuration of all other beliefs and
loyalties (particularly renunciation of any loyalty to the
new Catholic Faith), and an avowal of allegiance to the
horned god. Membership was contractual, that is, a
member signed an actual contract which limited her
obligations to the cult to a specific number of years,
at the end of which she was free to terminate allegiance.
Most often the Devil "promised her Mony, and that she
would live gallantly and have the pleasure of the
World . . ." [28] The neophyte's debts probably were paid
and she no doubt also learned the secrets of medicine,
drugs, telepathy, and simple sanitation, which would
have considerably improved all aspects of her earthly
existence. It was only according to the Church that she
lost her soul as part of the bargain. And, needless to
say, it was the Church, not the Devil, which took her life.

Once the neophyte made the decision for the
horned god, she went through a formal initiation, often
conducted at the sabbat. The ceremony was simple.
The initiate declared that she was joining the coven
of her own free will and swore devotion to the master

of the coven who represented the horned god. She was then marked with some kind of tattoo which was called the witches' mark. The inflicting of the tattoo was painful, and the healing process was long. When healed, the scar was red or blue and indelible. One method particularly favored by the witch hunters when hunting was to take a suspected woman, shave her pubic and other bodily hair (including head hair, eyebrows, etc.) and, upon finding any scar, find her guilty of witchcraft. Also, the existence of any supernumerary nipple, common in all mammals, was proof of guilt.

The initiate was often given a new name, especially if she had a Christian name like Mary or Faith. Children, when they reached puberty, were initiated into the coven — parents naturally wanted their children to share the family religion. The Inquisition was as ruthless with children as it was with adults. There are stories of children being whipped as their mothers were being burned — prevention, it was called.

The religious ceremony, which was the main content of the sabbat, included dancing, eating, and fucking. The worshipers paid homage to the horned god by kissing his representative, the master of the coven, anywhere he indicated. The kiss was generally on the master's ass — designed, some say, to provoke the antisodomy Christians. That ritual kiss was possibly placed on a mask which the costumed figure — masked, horned, wearing animal skins, and probably an artificial phallus — wore under his tail. The disguise conjures up the ancient, two-faced Janus.

The witches danced ring dances in a direction opposite to the path of the sun, an ancient, symbolic rite. The Lutherans and Puritans forbade dancing because it evoked for them the spectacle of pagan worship.

After the dancing, the witches ate. Often they brought their own food, rather in the tradition of picnic lunches, and sometimes the coven leader provided a real feast. The Christians alleged that the witches were cannibals and that their dinner was an orgy of human flesh, cooked and garnished as only the Devil knew how. Actually, the supper common to all sabbats was a simple meal of pedestrian food.

The whole notion of cannibalism and sacrifice has been stubbornly, persistently, and purposely misunderstood. There is no evidence that any living child was killed to be eaten, or that any living child was sacrificed. There is evidence that sometimes dead infants were ritually eaten, or used in ritual. Cannibalism, and its not so symbolic substitute, animal sacrifice, was a vital part of the ritual of all early religions, including the Jewish one. The witches participated in this tradition rather modestly: they generally sacrificed a goat or a hen. It was the Christians who developed and extended the Old World system of sacrifice and cannibalism to almost surreal ends: Christ, the sacrificial lamb, who died an agonizing death on the cross to ensure forgiveness of men's sins and whose followers symbolically, even today, eat of his flesh and drink of his blood—what is the Eucharist if not fossilized cannibalism?

The final activity of the sabbat was a phallic orgy— heathen, drug-abetted, communal sex. The sex of the sabbat is distinguished by descriptions of pain. It was said that intercourse was painful, that the phallus of the masked coven leader was cold and oversized, that no woman ever conceived. It would seem that the horned figure used an artificial phallus and could service all the celebrants. The Old Religion, as opposed to the Christian religion, celebrated sexuality, fertility, nature and woman's place in it, and communal sex was a logical and most sacral rite.

The worship of animals is also indigenous to nature-based religious systems. Early people existed among animals, scarcely distinct from them. Through religious ritual, people differentiated themselves from animals and gave honor to them — they were food, sustenance. There was a respect for the natural world — people were hunter and hunted simultaneously. Their perspective was acute. They worshiped the spirit and power they saw manifest in the carnivore world of which they were an integral part. When man began to be "civilized," to separate himself out of nature, to place himself over and above woman (he became Mind, she became Carnality) and other animals, he began to seek power over nature, magical control. The witch cults still had a strong sense of people as part of nature, and animals maintained a prime place in both ritual and consciousness for the witches. The Christians, who had a profound and compulsive hatred for the natural world, thought that the witches, through malice and a lust for power (pure projection, no doubt), had mobilized nature/animals into a robotlike anti-Christian army. The witch hunters were convinced that toads, rats, dogs, cats, mice, etc., took orders from witches, carried curses from one farm to another, caused death, hysteria, and disease. They thought that nature was one massive, crawling conspiracy against them, and that the conspiracy was organized and controlled by the wicked women. They can in fact be credited with pioneering the politics of total paranoia—they developed the classic model for that particular pathology which has, as its logical consequence, genocide. Their methods of dealing with the witch menace were developed empirically—they had a great respect for what worked. For instance, when they suspected a woman of witchcraft, they would lock her in an empty room for several days or weeks and if any living creature, any insect or spider, entered that room, that creature was identified as the woman's familiar, and she was proved guilty of witchcraft. Naturally, given the fact that bugs are everywhere, particularly in the woodwork, this test of guilt always worked.

Cats were particularly associated with witches. That association is based on the ancient totemic significance of the cat:

> It is well known that to the Egyptians cats were sacred. They were regarded as incarnations of Isis and there was also a cat deity. . . . Through Osiris (Ra) they were associated with the sun; the rays of the "solar cat," who was portrayed as killing the "serpent of darkness" at each dawn, were believed to produce fecundity in Nature, and thus cats were figures of fertility. . . . Cats were also associated with Hathor, a cow-headed goddess, and hence with crops and rain. . . .
>
> Still stronger, however, was the association of the cat with the moon, and thus she was a virgin goddess—a virgin-mother incarnation. In her character as moon-goddess she was inviolate and self-renewing . . . the circle she forms in a curled-up position [is seen as] the symbol for eternity, an unending re-creation.[29]

The Christians not only converted the horned god into Satan, but also the sacred cat into a demonic incarnation. The witches, in accepting familiars and particularly in their special feeling for cats, only participated in an ancient tradition which had as its substance love and respect for the natural world.

It was also believed that the witch could transform herself into a cat or other animal. This notion, called lycanthropy, is twofold:

> . . . either the belief that a witch or devil-ridden person temporarily assumes an animal form, to ravage or destroy; or, that they create an animal "double" in which, leaving the lifeless human body at home, he or she can wander, terrorize, or batten on mankind.[30]

The origins of the belief in lycanthropy can be traced to group rituals in which celebrants, costumed as animals, recreated animal movements, sounds, even hunting patterns. As group ritual, those celebrations would be prehistorical. The witches themselves, through the use of belladonna, aconite, and other drugs, felt that they did become animals.* The effect of the belief in lycanthropy on the general population was electric: a stray dog, a wild cat, a rat, a toad—all were witches, agents of Satan, bringing with them drought, disease, death. Any animal in the environment was dangerous, demonic. The legend of the werewolf (popularized in the Red Riding Hood fable) caused terror. At Labout,

---

*For a contemporary account of *lycanthropy*, I would suggest *The Teachings of Don Juan: A Yaqui Way of Knowledge*, by Carlos Castaneda (New York: Ballantine Books, 1968), pp. 170–84.

two hundred people were burned as werewolves. There
were endless stories of farmers shooting animals who
were plaguing them in the night, only to discover the
next morning that a respectable town matron had been
wounded in precisely the same way.

Witches, of course, could also fly on broomsticks,
and often did. Before going to the sabbat, they an-
nointed their bodies with a mixture of belladonna and
aconite, which caused delirium, hallucination, and gave
the sensation of flying. The broomstick was an almost
archetypal symbol of womanhood, as the pitchfork was
of manhood. Levitation was considered a rare but
genuine fact:

> As for its history, it is one of the earliest convic-
> tions, common to almost all peoples, that not only do
> supernatural beings, angels or devils, fly or float in the
> air at will, but so can those humans who invoke their
> assistance. Levitation among the saints was, and by the
> devout is, accepted as an objective fact. The most fa-
> mous instance is that of St. Joseph of Cupertino, whose
> ecstatic flights (and he perched in trees) caused em-
> barrassment in the seventeenth century. Yet the ap-
> pearance of flight, in celestial trance, has been claimed
> all through the history of the Church, and not only for
> such outstanding figures as St. Francis, St. Ignatius
> Loyola, or St. Teresa. . . . In the Middle Ages it was
> regarded as a marvel, but a firmly established one.
> . . . It is not, therefore, at all remarkable that witches
> were believed to fly . . . [though] the Church expressly
> forbade, during the reign of Charlemagne, any belief
> that witches flew.[31]

With typical consistency then, the Church said that
saints could fly but witches could not. As far as the

witches were concerned, they trusted their experience, they knew that they flew. Here they aligned themselves with Christian saints, yogis, mystics from all traditions, in the realization of a phenomenon so ancient that it would seem to extend almost to the origins of the religious impulse in people.

We now know most of what can be known about the witches: who they were, what they believed, what they did, the Church's vision of them. We have seen the historical dimensions of a myth of feminine evil which resulted in the slaughter of 9 million persons, nearly all women, over 300 years. The actual evidence of that slaughter, the remembrance of it, has been suppressed for centuries so that the myth of woman as the Original Criminal, the gaping, insatiable womb, could endure. Annihilated with the 9 million was a whole culture, woman-centered, nature-centered — all of their knowledge is gone, all of their knowing is destroyed. Historians (white, male, and utterly without credibility for women, Indians, Blacks, and other oppressed peoples as they begin to search the ashes of their own pasts) found the massacre of the witches too unimportant to include in the chronicles of those centuries except as a footnote, too unimportant to be seen as the substance of those centuries — they did not recognize the centuries of gynocide, they did not register the anguish of those deaths.

Our study of pornography, our living of life, tells us that the myth of feminine evil lived out so resolutely by the Christians of the Dark Ages, is alive and well, here and now. Our study of pornography, our living of life, tells us that though the witches are dead, burned alive at the stake, the belief in female evil is not, the hatred of female carnality is not. The Church has not changed its premises; the culture has not refuted those premises. It is left to us, the inheritors of that myth, to destroy it and the institutions based on it.

Part Four

ANDROGYNY

When the sexual energy of the people is liberated they will break the chains.

The struggle to break the form is paramount. Because we are otherwise contained in forms that deny us the possibility of realizing a form (a technique) to escape the fire in which we are being consumed.

The journey to love is not romantic.
Julian Beck, *The Life of the Theatre*

We want to destroy sexism, that is, polar role definitions of male and female, man and woman. We want to
destroy patriarchal power at its source, the family; in
its most hideous form, the nation-state. We want to
destroy the structure of culture as we know it, its art,
its churches, its laws: all of the images, institutions, and
structural mental sets which define women as hot wet
fuck tubes, hot slits.

Androgynous mythology provides us with a model
which does not use polar role definitions, where the
definitions are not, implicitly or explicitly, male = good,
female = bad, man = human, woman = other. Androgyny myths are multisexual mythological models. They
go well beyond bisexuality as we know it in the scenarios
they suggest for building community, for realizing the
fullest expression of human sexual possibility and
creativity.

Androgyny as a concept has no notion of sexual
repression built into it. Where woman is carnality, and
carnality is evil, it stands to reason (hail reason!) that
woman must be chained, whipped, punished, purged;
that fucking is shameful, forbidden, fearful, guilt-

ridden. Androgyny as the basis of sexual identity and community life provides no such imperatives. Sexual freedom and freedom for biological women, or all persons "female," are not separable. That they are different, and that sexual freedom has priority, is the worst of sexist hypes. Androgyny can show the way to both. It may be the one road to freedom open to women, men, and that emerging majority, the rest of us.

CHAPTER 8

Androgyny:
The Mythological Model

It is a question of finding the right model. We are born into a world in which sexual possibilities are narrowly circumscribed: Cinderella, Snow-white, Sleeping Beauty; O, Claire, Anne; romantic love and marriage; Adam and Eve, the Virgin Mary. These models are the substantive message of this culture—they define psychological sets and patterns of social interaction which, in our adult personae, we live out. We function inside the socioreligious scenario of right and wrong, good and bad, licit and illicit, legal and illegal, all saturated with shame and guilt. We are *programmed* by the culture as surely as rats are programmed to make the arduous way through the scientist's maze, and that programming operates on every level of choice and action. For example, we have seen how the romantic ethos is related to the way women dress and cosmeticize their bodies and how that behavior regulates the literal physical mobility of women. Take any aspect of behavior and one can find the source of the programmed response in the cultural structure. Western man's obsessive concern with metaphysical and political freedom is almost laughable in this context.

Depth psychologists consider man the center of his world — his psyche is the primary universe which governs, very directly, the secondary universe, distinct from him, of nature; philosophers consider man, in the fragmented, highly overrated part called intellect, the center of the natural world, indeed its only significant member; artists consider man, isolated in his creative function, the center of the creative process, of the canvas, of the poem, an engineer of the culture; politicians consider man, represented by his sociopolitical organization and its armies, the center of whatever planetary power might be relevant and meaningful; religionists consider God a surrogate man, created precisely in man's image, only more so, to be father to the human family. The notion of man as a part of the natural world, integrated into it, in form as distinct (no more so) as the tarantula, in function as important (no more so) as the honey bee or tree, is in eclipse, and that eclipse extends not over a decade, or over a century, but over the whole of written history. The arrogance which informs man's relation with nature (simply, he is superior to it) is precisely the same arrogance which informs his relationship with woman (simply, he is superior to her). Here we see the full equation: woman = carnality = nature. The separation of man from nature, man placing himself over and above it, is directly responsible for the current ecological situation which may lead to the extinction of many forms of life, including human life. Man has treated nature much as he has treated woman: with rape, plunder, violence. The phenomenological world is characterized by its diversity, the complexity and mutuality of its interactions, and man's only chance for survival in that world consists of finding the proper relationship to it.

In terms of interhuman relationship, the problem is similar. As individuals, we experience ourselves as the center of whatever social world we inhabit. We think that we are free and refuse to see that *we are functions of our particular culture.* That culture no longer organically reflects us, it is not our sum total, it is not the collective phenomenology of our creative possibilities—it possesses and rules us, reduces us, obstructs the flow of sexual and creative energy and activity, penetrates even into what Freud called the id, gives nightmare shape to natural desire. In order to achieve proper balance in interhuman interaction, we must find ways to change ourselves from culturally defined agents into naturally defined beings. We must find ways of destroying the cultural personae imposed on our psyches and we must discover forms of relationship, behavior, sexual being and interaction, which are compatible with our inherent natural possibilities. We must move away from the perverse, two-dimensional definitions which stem from sexual repression, which are the source of social oppression, and move toward creative, full, multidimensional modes of sexual expression.

Essentially the argument is this: we look at the world we inhabit and we see disaster everywhere; police states; prisons and mental hospitals filled to overflowing; alienation of workers from their work, women and men from each other, children from the adult community, governments contemptuous of their people, people filled with intense self-hatred; street violence, assault, rape, contract murderers, psychotic killers; acquisition gone mad, concentrated power and wealth; hunger, want, starvation, camps filled with refugees. Those phenomena mark the distance between civilized man and natural man, tribal man, whose sexual and social patterns functioned in a more integrated, balanced way. We know how it is now, and we want to know how it was then. While we cannot reconstruct the moment when humans emerged in evolution into recognizable humanness, or analyze that person to see what existence was like, while we cannot seek to emulate rituals and social forms of tribal people, or penetrate to and then imitate the dynamic relationship primitive people˙ had with the rest of the natural world, while we cannot even know much of what happened before people made pottery and built cities, while we cannot (and perhaps would not) obliterate the knowledge that we do have (of space travel and polio vaccines, cement and Hiroshima), we can still find extant in the culture echoes of a distant time when people were more together, figuratively and literally. These echoes reflect a period in human development when people functioned as a part of the natural world, not set over against it; when men and women, male and female, were whatever they were, not polar opposites, separated by dress and role into castes, fragmented pieces of some not-to-be-imagined whole.

In recent years, depth psychologists in particular have turned to primitive people and tribal situations in an effort to penetrate into the basic dynamics of male and female. The most notable effort was made by Jung, and it is necessary to state here that, admirable as his other work sometimes is, Jung and his followers have carried the baggage of patriarchy and sexual dualism with them into the search. Jung describes male and female in the absolute terms native to the culture, as archetypes preexistent in the psyche. Male is defined as authority, logic, order, that which is saturnian and embodies the consonant values of patriarchy; female is defined as emotional, receptive, anarchic, cancerian. Matriarchy preceded patriarchy because patriarchal values (particularly the need for complex organization) inform advanced societies, whereas female values inform more primitive tribal societies. As far as individual men and women are concerned, the male psyche has a feminine component (the subconscious) which is anarchic, emotional, sensitive, *lunar*, and the female personality has a male component (the conscious, or mind) which can be defined as a capacity for logical thought. Of course, biological women are ruled, it turns out, by the subconscious; men are ruled, not surprisingly, by the conscious, mind, intellect. One might imagine a time and place where intellect is not valued over anarchic, emotional, sensitive — looniness?: but that would be the most gratuitous kind of fantasy. Jung never questioned the cultural arbitrariness of these categories, never looked at them to see their political implications, never knew that they were sexist, that he functioned as an instrument of cultural oppression.

In the book *Woman's Mysteries: Ancient and Modern*, M. Esther Harding, a lifelong student of Jung and a Patron of the C. G. Jung Institute, applies Jungian ontology to a study of mythology. Taking the moon, Luna, as the patron saint of women (ignoring any masculine imagery associated with the moon, and this imagery is substantial; ignoring any feminine imagery connected with the sun, and this imagery is substantial), Harding ultimately identifies the female with the demonic, as did the Catholic Church:

> But if she will stop long enough to look within, she also may become aware of impulses and thoughts which are not in accord with her conscious attitudes but are the direct outcome of the crude and untamed feminine being within her. For the most part, however, a woman will not look at these dark secrets of her own nature. It is too painful, too undermining of the conscious character which she has built up for herself; she prefers to think that she really is as she appears to be. And indeed it is her task to stand between the Eros which is within her, and the world without, and through her own womanly adaptation to the world to make human, as it were, the daemoniac power of the nonhuman feminine principle.[1]

Eros, the subconscious, the flow of human sexual energy—described as the witch burners described it, "the daemoniac power of the nonhuman feminine principle." Harding is absolutely representative of the Jungian point of view.

It is a natural consequence of this dualistic stance that male and female are pitted against each other and that *conflict* is the dynamic mode of relationship open to male and female, men and women, when they meet:

> These discrepancies in their attitudes are dependent on the fact that the psychic constitution of men and women are essentially different; they are mirror opposites the one of the other. . . . So that their essential nature and values are diametrically opposed.[2]

These male and female sets are defined as archetypes, embedded in a collective unconscious, the given structure of reality. They are polar opposites; their mode of interaction is conflict. They cannot possibly understand each other because they are absolutely different: and of course, it is always easier to do violence to something Other, something whose "nature and values" are other. (Women have never understood that they are, by definition, Other, not male, therefore not human. But men do experience women as being totally opposite, other. How easy violence is.) There is, because Jung was a good man and Jungians are good people, a happy ending: though these two forces, male and female, are opposite, they are complementary, two halves of the same whole. One is not superior, one is not inferior. One is not good, one is not bad. But this resolution is inadequate because the culture, in its fiction and its history, demonstrates that one (male, logic, order, ego, father) is good and superior both, and that the other (guess which) is bad and inferior both. *It is the so-called female principle of Eros that all the paraphernalia of patriarchy conspires to suppress through the psychological, physiological, and economic oppression of those who are biologically women.* Jung's ontology serves those persons and institutions which subscribe to the myth of feminine evil.

The identification of the feminine with Eros, or erotic energy (carnality by any other name), comes from a fundamental misunderstanding of the nature of human sexuality. The essential information which would lead to nonsexist, nonrepressive notions of sexuality is to be found in androgyny myths, myths which

describe the creation of the first human being as male
and female in one form. In other words, Jung chose the
wrong model, the wrong myths, on which to construct
a psychology of male and female. He used myths in-
fused with patriarchal values, myths which gained currency in male-dominated cultures. The anthropological
discoveries which fueled the formation of his theories
all reveal relatively recent pieces of human history.
With few exceptions, all of the anthropological information we have deals with the near past.* But the myths
which are the foundation of and legitimize our culture
are gross perversions of original creation myths which
molded the psyches of earlier, possibly less self-con-
scious and more conscious, peoples. The original myths
all concern a primal androgyne — an androgynous godhead, an androgynous people. The corruptions of
these myths of a primal androgyne without exception
uphold patriarchal notions of sexual polarity, duality,
male and female as opposite and antagonistic. The
myth of a primal androgyne survives as part of a real
cultural underground: though it is ignored, despised
by a culture which posits other values, and though
those who relate their lifestyles directly to it have been
ostracized and persecuted.

With all of this talk of myth and mythology, what is
myth, and why does it have such importance? The best
definition remains that of Eliade, who wrote in *Myths,
Dreams, and Mysteries:*

---

* It is estimated that the time space between 7000 B.C. (when people
began to domesticate animals and make pottery) and 1974 A.D. is only 2 percent of the whole of human history.

What exactly is a myth? In the language current during the nineteenth century, a "myth" meant anything that was opposed to "reality": the creation of Adam, or the invisible man, no less than the history of the world as described by the Zulus, or the *Theogony* of Hesiod—these were all "myths." Like many another cliché of the Enlightenment and of Positivism, this, too, was of Christian origin and structure; for, according to primitive Christianity, everything which could not be justified by reference to one or the other of the two Testaments was untrue; it was a "fable." But the researches of the ethnologists have obliged us to go behind this semantic inheritance from the Christian polemics against the pagan world. We are at last beginning to know and understand the value of the myth, as it has been elaborated in "primitive" and archaic societies—that is, among those groups of mankind where the myth happens to be the very foundation of social life and culture. Now one fact strikes us immediately: in such societies the myth is thought to express the *absolute truth,* because it narrates a *sacred history;* that is, a transhuman revelation which took place at the dawn of the Great Time. . . . Being *real* and *sacred,* the myth becomes exemplary, and consequently, *repeatable,* for it serves as a model, and by the same token, a justification, for all human actions. In other words, *a myth is a true history of what came to pass at the beginning of Time, and one which provides the pattern for human behavior.*[3] [Italics added]

I would extend Eliade's definition in only one respect. It is not only in primitive and archaic societies that myths provide this model for behavior—it is in every human society. The distance between myth and social organization is perhaps greater, or more tangled, in advanced technological societies, but myth still operates

as the substructure of the collective. The story of Adam
and Eve will affect the shape of settlements on the moon
and Mars, and the Christian version of the primitive
myth of a divine fertility sacrifice saturates the most
technologically advanced communications media.

What are the myths of androgyny, and how do we
locate them behind the myths of polarity with which we
are familiar? Let us begin with the Chinese notions of yin
and yang.

Yin and yang are commonly associated with female
and male. The Chinese ontology, so appealing in that
it appears to give whole, harmonious, value-free description of phenomena, describes cosmic movement as
cyclical, thoroughly interwoven manifestation of yang
(masculine, aggressive, light, spring, summer) and yin
(female, passive, dark, fall, winter). The sexual identifi-
cations reduce the concepts too often to conceptual
polarities: they are used to fix the proper natures of
men and women as well as the forces of male and female.
These definitions, like the Jungian ones which are based
on them, are seemingly modified by the assertions that
(1) all people are composed of both yin and yang,
though in the man yang properly predominates and in
the woman yin properly predominates; (2) these male
and female forces are two parts of a whole, equally
vital, mutually indispensable. Unfortunately, as one
looks to day-to-day life, that biological incarnation of
yin, woman, finds herself, as always, the dark half of
the universe.

The sexual connotations of yin and yang, however,
are affixed onto the original concepts. They reflect an
already patriarchal, and misogynist, culture. Richard

Wilhelm, in an essay on an ancient Chinese text called *The Secret of the Golden Flower*, gives the uncorrupted meanings of yin and yang:

> Out of the Tao, and the *T'ai-chi* ["the great ridge pole, the supreme ultimate"] there develop the principles of reality, the one pole being the light (yang) and the other the dark, or the shadowy (yin). Among European scholars, some have turned first to sexual references for an explanation, but the characters refer to phenomena in nature. Yin is shade, therefore the north side of a mountain and the south side of a river. . . . Yang, in its original form, indicates flying pennants and, corresponding to the character of yin, is the south side of a mountain and the north side of a river. Starting only with the meaning of "light" and "dark," the principle was then expanded to all polar opposites, including the sexual. However, since both yin and yang have their common origin in an undivided One and are active only in the realm of phenomena, where yang appears as the active principle and conditions, and yin as the passive principle is derived and conditioned, it is quite clear that a metaphysical dualism is not the basis for these ideas.[4]

Light and dark are obvious in a phenomenological sense — there is day and it slowly changes into night which then slowly changes into day. When men began conceptualizing about the nature of the universe, the phenomena of light and dark were an obvious starting point. My own experience is that night and day are more alike than different — in which case they couldn't possibly be opposite. Man, in conceptualizing, has reduced phenomena to two, when phenomena are more complex and subtle than intellect can imagine.

Still, how is it that it is the feminine, the sexually female, that is embodied in yin? Even patriarchy and misogyny began somewhere. Here I can only guess. We know that at one time men were hunters and women were planters. Both forms of work were essential and arduous. Both demanded incredible physical strength and considerable knowledge and skill. Why did men hunt and women plant? Clearly women planted because they were often pregnant, and though pregnancy did not make them weak and passive, it did mean that they could not run, go without food for long periods of time, survive on the terms that hunting demanded. It is probable that very early in human history women also were hunters, and that it was crucial to the survival of the species that they develop into planters—first to supplement the food supply, second to reduce infant and woman mortality. We see that the first division of labor based on biological sex originated in a fundamental survival imperative. In the earliest of times, with no contraception and no notion of the place of the man in the process of impregnation, women were invested with a supreme magical power, one which engendered awe and fear in men. As they developed skill in planting, they embodied even more explicitly fertility, generation, and of course death. The overwhelming mana of women, coupled with the high mortality which went along with childbirth, could well have led to practices of protection, segregation, and slowly increasing social restriction. With pregnancy as the one inevitable in a woman's life, men began to organize social life in a way which excluded woman, which limited her to the living out of her reproductive function.

As men began to know power, that power directly related to the exclusion of women from community life, the myth of feminine evil developed and provided justification for laws, rites, and other practices which relegated women to pieces of property. As a corollary, men developed the taste for subjugating others and hoarding power and wealth which characterizes them to this very day.

Returning to yin and yang, what is crucial is the realization that these concepts did not originally attach to sex. In more concrete terms, the Great Original (first being) of the Chinese chronicles is the holy woman T'ai Yuan, who was an androgyne, a combined manifestation of yin and yang. Primacy is given to the feminine principle here (the gender of the noun is feminine) because of woman's generative function.

Among the Tibetan Buddhists, the so-called male-female polarities are called *yabyum*; among the Indian Hindus, they are called Shiva and Shakti. In the Tantric sects of both traditions, one finds a living religious cult attached to the myth of a primal androgyne, to the union of male and female. One also finds, not surprisingly, that Tantric cults are condemned by the parent culture with which they identify. The culminating religious rite of the Tantrics is sacramental fucking, the ritual union of man and woman which achieves, even if only symbolically, the original androgynous energy.

This is the outstanding fact when one looks at *yabyum* and Shiva-Shakti:

The Hindu assigned the male symbol apparatus to the passive, the female to the active pole; the Buddhist did

the opposite; the Hindu assigned the knowledge principle to the passive male pole, and the dynamic principle to the active female pole; the Vajrayana Buddhist
did it the other way around.[5]

The explanation for this major difference, this attach-
ment in one case of the feminine to the passive and in
the other of the feminine to the active, is that these
attachments were made *arbitrarily.*[6] Two convictions
vital to sexist ontology are undermined: that everywhere the feminine is synonymous with the passive,
receptive, etc., and so it must be true; that the definition of the feminine as passive, receptive, etc., comes
from the visible, incontrovertible fact of feminine passivity, receptivity, etc.

In Hindu mythology, as opposed to Judaic mythology, the phenomenological world is not created by
god as something distinct from him. It is the godhead
in manifestation. As Campbell describes it: ". . . the
image of the androgynous ancestor is developed in
terms of an essentially psychological reading of the
problem of creation." [7] In a description of that androgynous being, we find: "He was just as large as a man and
woman embracing. This Self then divided himself into
two parts; and with that there was a master and a
mistress. Therefore this body, by itself, as the sage
Yajnavalkya declares, is like half of a split pea." [8]

In Egypt one of the earliest forms of moon deity was
Isis-Net, an androgyne. The Greek Artemis was an-
drogynous. So is Awonawilona, chief god of the Pueblo
Zuni. The Greek god Eros was also androgynous.

Plato, repeating a corrupted version of a much

older myth, describes in *Symposium* 3 types of original human beings: male/male, male/female, female/
female. These original humans were so powerful that
the gods feared them and so Zeus, whose own androgynous ancestry did not stop him from becoming the
Macho Kid, halved them.

The Aranda of Australia know a supernatural being
called Numbakulla, "Eternal," who made androgynes
as the first beings, then split them apart, then tied them
back together with hemp to make couples. It is essentially this story that is repeated throughout the primitive world.

Certain African and Melanesian tribes have ances-
tral images of one being with breasts, penis, and beard.
Hindu statues which show Shiva and Shakti united participate in the same devotional tradition — we perceive
that they are united in sexual intercourse, but it is
also possible that they represent one literal androgynous body.

There are still devotional religious practices which
harken back to the mythology of the primal androgyne
— Tantra, for instance, in both its Tibetan and Indian
manifestations, clearly participates in that tradition.
Possibly the rite of subincision, practiced in Australia,
is similarly rooted in androgyne myth. Subincision is the
ritual slitting open of the underside of the penis to form
a permanent cleft into the urethra. The opening is
called the "penis womb." Campbell notes that "The
subincision produces artificially a hypospadias resem-
bling that of a certain class of hermaphrodites." [9]
The drive back to androgyny, where it is manifest, is
sacral, strong, compelling. It is interesting here to

speculate on the incest taboo. The Freudian articulation
of what the Oedipal complex is and means serves the
imperatives of a patriarchal culture, of Judeo-Christian morality, and remains largely unchallenged. But
the earliest *devotional* mother-son configurations are
those of a Mother/Goddess and her Son/Lover. The
son is lover to the mother and is ritually sacrificed at a
predetermined time (mothers don't have to be posses-
sive). This sacrifice is not related to guilt or punishment—it is holy sacrifice which sanctifies the tribe, does
honor to the offering, and is premised on cyclic fertility patterns of life, death, and regeneration. These
rites, associated with the worship of the Great Mother
(the first corruption of the Great Original, or primal
androgyne) involved ritual intercourse between mother
and son, with the subsequent sacrifice of the son. At
one time both a son and a daughter were sacrificed, but
as the daughter became a mother-surrogate, the son
was sacrificed alone. This sacralized set, Mother/God-
dess–Son/Lover, and the rituals associated with it, are
postandrogyne developments: that is, men and women
experienced separateness (not duality) and attempted
to recreate symbolically the androgynous state of mind
and body through what we now call incest. If it is true
that the implications of the androgyny myths in terms
of behavior run counter to every Judeo-Christian, or
more generally sexist, notion of morality, it would follow that incest is the primary taboo of this and similar
cultures because it has its roots in the sexually dynamic
androgynous mentality. Indeed, it is not surprising
to discover that early versions of the Oedipus story do
not end with Oedipus putting his eyes out. Sophocles

leaves Oedipus overcome with fear, guilt, and remorse, blinded and ruined. In the earlier Homeric version, Oedipus becomes king and reigns happily ever after. Freud chose the wrong version of the right story.

Even Jewish mythology provides a primal androgyne. Here is the substance of a cultural underground most directly related to us. According to the Zohar, the first created woman was not Eve but Lilith. She was created coterminous with Adam, that is, they were created in one body, androgynous. They were of one substance, one corporality. God, so the legend goes, split them apart so that Lilith could be dressed as a bride and married to Adam properly, but Lilith rebelled at the whole concept of marriage, that is, of being defined as Adam's inferior, and fled. Lilith was in fact the first woman and the first feminist both. The Jewish patriarchs, with shrewd vengeance, called her a witch. They said that the witch Lilith haunted the night (her name is etymologically associated with the Hebrew word for night) and killed infants. She became symbolic of the dark, evil side of all women. Of course, Lilith, we know now, made the correct analysis and went to the core of the problem: she rejected the nuclear family. God, however, saw it differently—he had created Lilith from dust, just as he had created Adam. He had created her free and equal. Not making the same mistake twice, Eve was created from Adam's rib, clearly giving her no claim to either freedom or equality. It took the Christians to assert that since the rib is bent, woman's nature is contrary to man's.

How then can we understand the biblical statement that God created man in his own image—male and fe-

male created he them? The Midrash gives the definitive answer: *When the Holy One, Blessed Be He, created
the first man, he created him androgynous.*[10] There is also
a corresponding Jewish androgynous godhead. The
very word for the godhead, *Elohim,* is composed of a
feminine noun and a masculine plural ending. God
is multiple and androgynous. The tradition of the
androgynous godhead is most clearly articulated in the
Kabbalah, a text which in written form goes back to the
Middle Ages. The oral Kabbalah, which is more extensive than the written Kabbalah, originates in the
most obscure reaches of Jewish history, before the
Bible, and has been preserved with, according to oc-
cultists, more care than the written Bible — that is, the
Bible has been rewritten, edited, modified, translated;
oral Kabbalah has retained its purity.

The Kabbalistic scheme of the godhead is complex.
Suffice it here to say that god is male and female interwoven. Certain parts are associated with the female,
other parts with the male. For instance, primal understanding is female; wisdom is male; severity is female;
mercy is male. Special prominence is given to the final
emanation of the godhead, Malkuth the Queen, the
physical manifestation of the godhead in the universe.
Malkuth the Queen is roughly equivalent to Shakti. For
the Kabbalists, as for the Tantrics, the ultimate sacrament is sexual intercourse which recreates androgyny.
Just as the Tantrics are/were ostracized by the rest of
the Hindu and Buddhist communities, so do the main
body of Jews ostracize the Kabbalists. Now they are
considered to be freaks — they have been viewed as
heretics. And heretics they are, for in recognizing the

androgynous nature of the godhead they undermine the authority of God the Father and threaten the power of patriarchy.

It remains only to point out that Christ also had some notion of androgyny. In Gospel to the Egyptians, Christ and a disciple named Salomé have this conversation:

> When Salomé asked how long Death should prevail, the Lord said: So long as ye women bear children; for I have come to destroy the work of the Female. And Salomé said to Him: Did I therefore well in having no children? The Lord answered and said: Eat every Herb, but eat not that which hath bitterness. When Salomé asked when these things about which she questioned would be made known, the Lord said: When ye trample upon the garment of shame; when the Two become One, and Male with Female neither male nor female.[11]

In the next chapter I am going to pursue the implications of androgyny myths in the areas of sexual identity and sexual behavior, and it would be in keeping with the spirit of this book to take Christ as my guide and say with him: "When ye trample upon the garment of shame; when the Two become One, and Male with Female neither male nor female."

CHAPTER 9

Androgyny: Androgyny, Fucking, and Community

Nothing short of everything will really do.
Aldous Huxley, *Island*

The discovery is, of course, that "man" and "woman" are fictions, caricatures, cultural constructs. As models they are reductive, totalitarian, inappropriate to human becoming. As roles they are static, demeaning to the female, dead-ended for male and female both. Culture as we know it legislates those fictive roles as normalcy. Deviations from sanctioned, sacred behavior are "gender disorders," "criminality," as well as "sick," "disgusting," and "immoral." Heterosexuality, which is properly defined as the ritualized behavior built on polar role definition, and the social institutions related to it (marriage, the family, the Church, *ad infinitum*) are "human nature." Homosexuality, transsexuality, incest, and bestiality persist as the "perversions" of this "human nature" we presume to know so much about. They persist despite the overwhelming forces marshaled against them — discriminatory laws and social practices, ostracism, active persecution by the state and other organs of the culture — as inexplicable embarrassments, as odious examples of "filth" and/or "maladjustment." The attempt here, however modest and incomplete, is to discern another ontology, one which discards the fiction that there are two polar distinct sexes.

We have seen that androgyny myths present an image of one corporality which is both male and female. Sometimes the image is literally a man-form and a woman-form in one body. Sometimes it is a figure which incorporates both male and female functions. In every case, that mythological image is a paradigm for a wholeness, a harmony, and a freedom which is virtually unimaginable, the antithesis of every assumption we hold about the nature of identity in general and sex in particular. The first question then is: What of biology? There are, after all, men and women. They are different, demonstrably so. We are each of one sex or the other. If there are two discrete biological sexes, then it is not hard to argue that there are two discrete modes of human behavior, sex-related, sex-determined. One might argue for a liberalization of sex-based roles, but one cannot justifiably argue for their total redefinition.

Hormone and chromosome research, attempts to develop new means of human reproduction (life created in, or considerably supported by, the scientist's laboratory), work with transsexuals, and studies of formation of gender identity in children provide basic information which challenges the notion that there are two discrete biological sexes. That information threatens to transform the traditional biology of sex difference into the radical biology of sex similarity. That is not to say that there is one sex, but that there are many. The evidence which is germane here is simple. The words "male" and "female," "man" and "woman," are used only because as yet there are no others.

1. Men and women have the same basic body structure. Both have both male and female genitals — the clitoris is a vestigial penis, the prostate gland is most probably a vestigial womb. Since, as I pointed out earlier, there is information on only 2 percent of human history, and since religious chronicles, which were for centuries the only record of human history, consistently speak of another time in the cycle of time when humans were androgynous, and since each sex has the vestigial organs of the other, there is no reason not to postulate that humans once were androgynous — hermaphroditic and androgynous, created precisely in the image of that constantly recurring androgynous godhead.

2. Until the 7th week of fetal development both sexes have precisely the same external genitalia. Basically, the development of sex organs and ducts is the same for males and females and the same two sets of ducts develop in both.

3. The gonads cannot be said to be entirely male or female. Dr. Mary Jane Sherfey writes:

> In their somatic organization, the gonads always retain a greater or lesser amount of the opposite-sex tissue which remains functional throughout life.[1]

4. Chromosomal sex is not necessarily the visible sex of the individual. It happens that a person of one

chromosomal sex develops the gonads of the other sex.*
Gonadal sex and chromosomal sex can be in direct contradiction.

5. Chromosomal sex is not only XX or XY. There are other chromosomal formations, and not much is known about them or what they signify.

6. A person can have the gonads of one sex, and the secondary sexual characteristics of the other sex.

7. Men and women both produce male and female hormones. The amounts and proportions vary greatly, and there is no way to determine biological maleness or femaleness from hormone count.

8. One hormone can be transformed by the body into its "opposite," male into female, female into male. In *Sex, Gender, and Society,* Ann Oakley gives this example:

> . . . the fact that rapidly maturing male adolescents sometimes acquire small breasts—the substantial increases in testosterone which accompanies puberty [are] partially metabolised as oestrogen, which in turn causes breast development.[2]

9. It is now thought that the male hormone determines the sex drive in both men and women.

---

*Question: Can a person with the chromosomal sex of a male and the gonadal sex of a female conceive? If so, we would have to accept the notion that men can have children. I would think that such cases do exist in nature, even though I could find no confirmation that such persons are fertile. Since anyone who has children is defined as a woman, and chromosome tests are not done routinely, such persons would probably not be discovered except by accident.

10. The female hormone (progesterone) can have a masculinizing effect. Dr. Sherfey writes:

> We may have difficulty conceiving it, but natural se-
> lection has no difficulty using sexually heterotypic
> structures for homotypic purposes. For example,
> progesterone is the "pregnancy hormone" essential
> for menstruation and the prolonged pregnancy. It is as
> uniquely a "female" hormone as one can be. Yet pro-
> gesterone possesses strong androgenic properties. It
> may be used to masculinize female embryos. In 1960,
> Jones (27, 63) demonstrated that progesterone given
> to human mothers early in pregnancy to prevent
> threatened miscarriages . . . severely masculinized a
> female fetus.[3]

11. Visible sex differences are not discrete. There are men with tiny cocks, women with large clits. There are men with highly developed breasts, women with almost no breast development. There are men with wide hips, women with no noticeable hip development. There are men with virtually no body hair, women with much body hair. There are men with high voices, women with low voices. There are men with no facial hair, women who have beards and mustaches.

12. Height and weight differences between men and women are not discrete. Muscle structures are not dis-crete. We know the despair of the tall, muscular woman who does not fit the female stereotype; we know also the despair of the small, delicate man who does not fit the male stereotype.

13. There is compelling cross-cultural evidence that muscle strength and development are culturally deter-

mined. There are cultures in which there are no great differences in somatotype of men and women:

> In one small-scale ("primitive") society for which there are good photographic records—the Manus of the Admiralty Islands—there is apparently no difference at all in somatotype between males and females as children, and as adults both men and women tend to the same high degree of mesomorphy (broad shoulders and chest, heavily muscled limbs, little subcutaneous fat). . . . In Bali, too, males and females lack the sort of differentiation of the physique that is a visible difference in our culture. Geoffrey Gorer once described them as a "hermaphroditic" people; they have little sex differential in height and both sexes have broad shoulders and narrow hips. They do not run to curves and muscles, to body hair or to breasts of any size. (Gorer once remarked that you could not tell male and female apart, even from the front.) Another source informs us that babies suck their fathers' breasts as well as their mothers'.[4]

14. There are hermaphrodites in nature. Robert T. Francoeur, in *Utopian Motherhood: New Trends in Human Reproduction*, admits:

> The medical profession and experimental biologists have always been very skeptical about the existence of functional hermaphrodites among the higher animals and man, though the earthworm, the sea hare, and other lower animals do combine both sexes in the same individual.[5]

We have seen how deep the commitment to human sexual discreteness and polarity goes—that commitment makes the idea of functional hermaphroditism conceptually intolerable. It is interesting here to speculate on the perceptions of men like Lionel Tiger (*Men in Groups*) who in effect project human cultural patterns of dominance and submission on the animal world. For instance, Dr. Sherfey tells us that *"In many primate species, the females would be diagnosed hermaphrodites if they were human."* (Italics hers.) [6] Most probably, we often simply project our own culturally determined modes of acting and perceiving onto other animals — we effectively screen information that would challenge the notions of male and female which are holy to us. In that case, a bias toward androgyny (instead of the current bias toward polarity) would give us significantly different scenarios of animal behavior.

Hermaphroditism is generally defined as "a congenital disorder in which both male and female generative organs exist in the same individual." [7] A "true" hermaphrodite is one who has ovaries, testes, and the secondary sexual characteristics of both sexes. But this is, it seems to me, the story of a functional hermaphrodite:

> The case involved a sixteen-year-old Arkansas girl who was being operated on for an ovarian tumor. As is the custom in such surgery, the tissue removed is carefully examined by a pathologist. In this instance, signs of live eggs *and* live sperm were found in different regions of the tumor. With the egg and the sperm situated right next to each other in the same organ, Dr. Timme claimed "there was a great possibility that they would combine and make a human being." . . . The unique feature . . . would be that the *same* person contributed *both* germ cells. [8]

Parthenogenesis also occurs naturally in women. Francoeur refers to the work of Dr. Landrum B. Shettles who

> in examining human eggs just after they were removed from their ovarian follicles . . . found that three out of four hundred of these eggs had "undergone cleavage *in vivo* within the intact follicle, without any possible contact with spermatozoa." [9]

On the basis of Shettles' work, Francoeur estimates

> that virgin births are a rather common occurrence, in about the same frequency as fraternal twins and twice as often as identical twins occur among white Americans. [10]

Seemingly a conservative, Dr. Sherwood Taylor, a British scientist, "has suggested a much lower frequency for human parthenogenesis, estimating one case in ten thousand births." [11] However much, however little, it does occur.

We can presume then that there is a great deal about human sexuality to be discovered, and that our notion of two discrete biological sexes cannot remain intact. We can presume then that we will discover cross-sexed phenomena in proportion to our ability to see them. In addition, we can account for the relative rarity of hermaphrodites in the general population, for the consistency of male-female somatotypes that we do find, and for the relative rarity of cross-sexed characteristics in the general population (though they occur with more frequency than we are now willing to imagine) by recognizing that there is a process of *cultural selec-*

tion which, for people, supersedes natural selection in importance. Cultural selection, as opposed to natural selection, does not necessarily serve to improve the species or to ensure survival. It does necessarily serve to uphold cultural norms and to ensure that deviant somatotypes and cross-sexed characteristics are systematically bred out of the population.

However we look at it, whatever we choose to make out of the data of what is frequently called Intersex, it is clear that sex determination is not always clearcut and simple. Dr. John Money of Johns Hopkins University has basically isolated these six aspects of sex identity:

1. *Genetic or nuclear sexuality* as revealed by indicators like the sex-chromatin or Barr-body, a full chromosomal count and the leucocytic drumstick; *

2. *Hormonal sexuality* which results from a balance that is predominantly androgenic or estrogenic;

3. *Gonadal sexuality* which may be clearly ovarian or testicular, but occasionally also mixed;

4. *Internal sexuality* as disclosed in the structure of the internal reproductive system;

5. *External genital sexuality* as revealed in the external anatomy, and finally;

6. *Psychosexual development* which through the external forces of rearing and social conditioning along with the individual's response to these factors directs the development of a personality which is by nature sexual.[12]

* An object in the cell itself which would seem to determine gender.

Since there can be total contradiction between/ among any of the above, since we have discussed some (by no means all) of the cross-sexed characteristics of human biological functioning, since we recognize hermaphroditism and parthenogenesis as human realities, we are justified in making a radical new formulation of the nature of human sexuality. *We are, clearly, a multi-sexed species which has its sexuality spread along a vast fluid continuum where the elements called male and female are not discrete.**

The concrete implications of multisexuality as we find it articulated in both androgynous mythology and biology necessitate the total redefinition of scenarios of proper human sexual behavior and pragmatic forms of human community. If human beings are multisexed, then all forms of sexual interaction which are directly rooted in the multisexual nature of people must be part of the fabric of human life, accepted into the lexicon of human possibility, integrated into the forms of human community. By redefining human sexuality, or by defining it correctly, we can transform human relationship and the institutions which seek to control that relationship. Sex as the power dynamic between men and women, its primary form sadomasochism, is what we know now. Sex as community between humans, our shared humanity, is the world we must build. What

---

* The notion of bisexuality is organically rooted to structural polarity and is inappropriate here for these reasons: the word itself has duality built into it; one can be bisexual and still relate to the fictions "male" and "female" —to both instead of to one; one can be bisexual and still relate exclusively to one role, the masculine or the feminine, whether found in men or women.

kind of sexual identity and relation will be the substance of that community?

Heterosexuality and Homosexuality.*

> There are men I could spend eternity with,
> But not this life.
>
> Kathleen Norris

> a little zen in our politics a little acid in
> our tea, could be all we need. the poof
> is in the putting.
>
> Jill Johnston

I have defined heterosexuality as the ritualized behavior built on polar role definition. Intercourse with men as we know them is increasingly impossible. It requires an aborting of creativity and strength, a refusal of responsibility and freedom: a bitter personal death. It means remaining the victim, forever annihilating all self-respect. It means acting out the female role, incorporating the masochism, self-hatred, and passivity which are central to it. Unambiguous conventional heterosexual behavior is the worst betrayal of our common humanity.

That is not to say that "men" and "women" should not fuck. Any sexual coming together which is genuinely pansexual and role-free, even if between men and women as we generally think of them (i.e., the biological images we have of them), is authentic and androgynous. Specifically, *androgynous fucking requires the destruction*

---

* For bisexuality, cf. p. 183.

*of all conventional role-playing, of genital sexuality as the
primary focus and value, of couple formations, and of the
personality structures dominant-active ("male") and sub-
missive-passive ("female").*

Homosexuality, because it is by definition antagonistic to two-sex polarity, is closer at its inception
to androgynous sexuality. However, since all individual
consciousness and social relationship are polluted by
internalized notions of polarity, coupling, and role-
playing, the criteria cited above must also be applied to
homosexual relation. Too often homosexual relation
transgresses gender imperatives without transforming
them.

An exclusive commitment to one sexual formation,
whether homosexual or heterosexual, generally means
an exclusive commitment to one role. An exclusive
commitment to one sexual formation generally involves the denial of many profound and compelling
kinds of sensuality. An exclusive commitment to one
sexual formation generally means that one is, regardless of the uniform one wears, a good soldier of the
culture programmed effectively to do its dirty work.
It is by developing one's pansexuality to its limits
(and no one knows where or what those are) that one
does the work of destroying culture to build community.

Transsexuality

How can I really care if we win "the Revolution"? Either way, any way, there will be
no place for me.
A transsexual friend, in a conversation

Transsexuality is currently considered a gender disorder, that is, a person learns a gender role which contradicts his/her visible sex. It is a "disease" with a cure: a sex-change operation will change the person's visible sex and make it consonant with the person's felt identity.

Since we know very little about sex identity, and since psychiatrists are committed to the propagation of the cultural structure as it is, it would be premature and not very intelligent to accept the psychiatric judgment that transsexuality is caused by faulty socialization. More probably transsexuality is caused by a faulty society. Transsexuality can be defined as one particular formation of our general multisexuality which is unable to achieve its natural development because of extremely adverse social conditions.

There is no doubt that in the culture of male-female discreteness, transsexuality is a disaster for the individual transsexual. Every transsexual, white, black, man, woman, rich, poor, is in a state of primary emergency (see p. 185) as a transsexual. There are 3 crucial points here. One, every transsexual has the right to survival on his/her own terms. That means that every transsexual is entitled to a sex-change operation, and it should be provided by the community as one of its functions. This is an emergency measure for an emergency condition. Two, by changing our premises about men and women, role-playing, and polarity, the social situation of transsexuals will be transformed, and transsexuals will be integrated into community, no longer persecuted and despised. Three, community built on androgynous identity will mean the end of transsexuality as we know it. Either the transsexual will be able to expand his/her sexuality into a fluid androgyny, or, as roles disappear, the phenomenon of transsexuality will disappear and that energy will be transformed into new modes of sexual identity and behavior.

Transvestism

> The first time I put on the black silk
> panties I got a hardon right away.
> Julian Beck

Transvestism is costuming which violates gender imperatives. Transvestism is generally a sexually charged act: the visible, public violation of sex role is erotic, exciting, dangerous. It is a kind of erotic civil disobedience, and that is precisely its value. Costuming is part of the strategy and process of role destruction. We see, for instance, that as women reject the female role, they adopt "male" clothing. As sex roles dissolve, the particular erotic content of transvestism dissolves.

Bestiality

> [In the Middle Ages] copulation with a
> Jew was regarded as a form of bestiality,
> and incurred the same penances.
> G. Rattray-Taylor, *Sex in History*

Primary bestiality (fucking between people and other animals) is found in all nonindustrial societies. Secondary bestiality (generalized erotic relationships between people and other animals) is found everywhere on the planet, on every city street, in every rural town. Bestiality is an erotic reality, one which clearly places people in nature, not above it.

The relationship between people and other animals, when nonpredatory, is always erotic since its substance is nonverbal communication and touch. That eroticism in its pure form is life-affirming and life-enriching was sufficient reason to make bestiality a capital crime in the Dark Ages, at least for the nonhuman animal; sufficient reason for the English in the Dark Ages to confuse sheep and Jews.

In contemporary society relationships between people and other animals often reflect the sadomasochistic complexion of human relationship. Animals in our culture are often badly abused, the objects of violence and cruelty, the foil of repressed and therefore very dangerous human sexuality. Some animals, like horses and big dogs, become surrogate cocks, symbols of ideal macho virility.

Needless to say, in androgynous community, human and other-animal relationships would become more explicitly erotic, and that eroticism would not degenerate into abuse. Animals would be part of the tribe and, with us, respected, loved, and free. They always share our fate, whatever it is.

Incest

> I was cold—later revolted a little, not much—seemed perhaps a good idea to try —know the Monster of the Beginning Womb—Perhaps—that way. Would she care? She needs a lover.
>
> Allen Ginsberg, *Kaddish*

The parent-child relationship is primarily erotic because all human relationships are primarily erotic. The incest taboo is a particularized form of repression, one which functions as the bulwark of all the other repressions. The incest taboo ensures that however free we become, we never become genuinely free. The incest taboo, because it denies us essential fulfillment with the parents whom we love with our primary energy, forces us to internalize those parents and constantly seek them, or seek to negate them, in the minds, bodies, and hearts of other humans who are not our parents and never will be.

The incest taboo does the worst work of the culture: it teaches us the mechanisms of repressing and internalizing erotic feeling—it forces us to develop those mechanisms in the first place; it forces us to particularize sexual feeling, so that it congeals into a need for a particular sexual "object"; it demands that we place the nuclear family above the human family. The destruction of the incest taboo is essential to the development of cooperative human community based on the free-flow of natural androgynous eroticism.

The Family

> For if we grant that the sexual drive is at birth diffuse and undifferentiated from the total personality (Freud's "polymorphous perversity") and . . . becomes differentiated only in response to the incest taboo; and that . . . the incest taboo is now necessary only in order to preserve the family; then if we did away with the family we would in effect be doing away with the

> repressions that mold sexuality into specific formations.
>
> Shulamith Firestone,
> *The Dialectic of Sex*

The incest taboo can be destroyed only by destroying the nuclear family as the primary institution of the culture. The nuclear family is the school of values in a sexist, sexually repressed society. One learns what one must know: the roles, rituals, and behaviors appropriate to male-female polarity and the internalized mechanisms of sexual repression. The alternative to the nuclear family at the moment is the extended family, or tribe. The growth of tribe is part of the process of destroying particularized roles and fixed erotic identity. As people develop fluid androgynous identity, they will also develop the forms of community appropriate to it. We cannot really imagine what those forms will be.

Children

> The special tie women have with children is recognized by everyone. I submit, however, that the nature of this bond is no more than shared oppression. And that moreover this oppression is intertwined and mutually reinforcing in such complex ways that we will be unable to speak of the liberation of women without also discussing the liberation of children.
>
> Shulamith Firestone,
> *The Dialectic of Sex*

Two developments are occurring simultaneously: women are rejecting the female role, and life is being created in the laboratory. Unless the structure is totally transformed, we can expect that when women no longer function as biological breeders we will be expendable. As *men* learn more and more to control reproduction, as cloning becomes a reality, and as the technology of computers and robots develop, there is every reason to think that men as we know them will use that control and technology to create the sex objects that will gratify them. Men, after all, have throughout history resorted to gynocide as a stratagem of social control, as a tactical way of attaining/maintaining power. That is the simple, compelling reality. There are only two other options: women must seize power, or we must accomplish the transformation into androgyny.

The freedom of those who are capable of biological reproduction from that work (which is simply a form of physical labor) is entirely congruent with androgynous community. Only in the concentration-camp world of polarity must one expect that development to lead to gynocide. The social processes here stand naked: if women must seize power in order to survive, and somehow manage to do that, power will most probably shift without being transformed; if we can create androgynous community, we can abandon power altogether as a social reality—that is the final, and most important, implication of androgyny.

As for children, they too are erotic beings, closer to androgyny than the adults who oppress them. Children are fully capable of participating in community, and have every right to live out their own erotic impulses. In androgynous community, those impulses would retain a high degree of nonspecificity and would no doubt show the rest of us the way into sexual self-realization. The distinctions between "children" and "adults," and the social institutions which enforce those distinctions, would disappear as androgynous community develops.

Conclusion

> Nothing short of everything will really do.
> Aldous Huxley, *Island*

The object is cultural transformation. The object is the development of a new kind of human being and a new kind of human community. All of us who have ever tried to right a wrong recognize that truly nothing short of everything will really do.

The way from here to there will not be easy. We must make a total commitment—no longer to take refuge in the scenarios of man-woman violence which are society's regulators, no longer to play the male-female roles we have been taught, no longer to refuse to know who we are and what we desire so that we need not take responsibility for our own lives. We must refuse to submit to those institutions which are by definition sexist—marriage, the nuclear family, religions built on the myth of feminine evil. We must refuse to submit to the fears engendered by sexual taboos. We must refuse to submit to all forms of behavior and relationship which reinforce male-female polarity, which nourish basic patterns of male dominance and female submission. We must instead build communities where violence is not the main dynamic of human relationship, where natural desire is the fundament of community, where androgyny is the operative premise, where tribe based on androgyny and the social forms which would develop from it are the bases of the collective cultural structure — noncoercive, nonsexist. As Julian Beck wrote, the journey to love is not romantic. As many have written, the journey to freedom is not romantic either — nor is the way known precisely and for all time. We begin here and now, inch by inch.

You do not teach someone to count only up to eight. You do not say nine and ten and beyond do not exist. You give people everything or they are not able to count at all. There is a real revolution or none at all.

Pericles Korovessis, in an interview in *Liberation*, June 1973

The Revolution is not an event that takes two or three days, in which there is shooting and hanging. It is a long drawn out process in which new people are created, capable of renovating society so that the revolution does not replace one elite with another, but so that the revolution creates a new anti-authoritarian structure with anti-authoritarian people who in their turn re-organize the society so that it becomes a non-alienated human society, free from war, hunger, and exploitation.

Rudi Dutschke, March 7, 1968

There is a misery of the body and a misery of the mind, and if the stars, whenever we looked at them, poured nectar into our mouths, and the grass became bread, we would still be sad. We live in a system that manufactures sorrow, spilling it out of its mill, the waters of sorrow, ocean, storm, and we drown down, dead, too soon.

. . . uprising is the reversal of the system, and revolution is the turning of tides.
Julian Beck, *The Life of the Theatre*

AFTERWORD
The Great Punctuation Typography Struggle

---

this text has been altered in one very serious way. I wanted it to be printed the way it was written—lower case letters, no apostrophes, contractions.

I like my text to be as empty as possible. only necessary punctuation is necessary. when one knows ones purposes one knows what is necessary.

my publisher, in his corporate wisdom, filled the pages with garbage: standard punctuation. he knew his purposes; he knew what was necessary. our purposes differed: mine, to achieve clarity; his, to sell books.

my publisher changed my punctuation because book reviewers (Mammon) do not like lower case letters.

fuck (in the old sense) book reviewers (Mammon).

When I say god and mammon concerning the writer writing, I mean that any one can use words to say something. And in using these words to say what he has to say he may use those words directly or indirectly. If he uses these words indirectly he says what he intends to have heard by somebody who is to hear and in so doing inevitably he has to serve mammon. . . . Now serving god for a writer who is writing is writing anything directly, it makes no difference what it is but

187

it must be direct, the relation between the thing done
and the doer must be direct. In this way there is com-
pletion and the essence of the completed thing is com-
pletion.

Gertrude Stein

in a letter to me, Grace Paley wrote, "once everyone
tells the truth artists will be unnecessary—meanwhile
there's work for us."

telling the truth. we know what it is when we do it
and when we learn not to do it we forget what it is.

form. shape, structure, spatial relation, how the
printed word appears on the page, where to breathe,
where to rest. punctuation is marking time, indicating
rhythms. even in my original text I used too much of it
—I overorchestrated. I forced you to breathe where I
do, instead of letting you discover your own natural
breath.

I begin by presuming that I am free.

I begin with nothing, no form, no content, and I ask:
what do I want to do and how do I want to do it.

I begin by presuming that what I write belongs to
me.

I begin by presuming that I determine the form I
use—in all its particulars. I work at my craft—in all
its particulars.

in fact, everything is already determined.

in fact, all the particulars have been determined and
are enforced.

in fact, where I violate what has already been determined I will be stopped.

in fact, the enforcers will enforce.

"Whatever he may seem to us, he is yet a servant of the Law; that is, he belongs to the Law and as such is set beyond human judgment. In that case one dare not believe that the doorkeeper is subordinate to the man. Bound as he is by his service, even at the door of the Law, he is incomparably freer than anyone at large in the world. The man is only seeking the Law, the doorkeeper is already attached to it. It is the Law that has placed him at his post; to doubt his integrity is to doubt the Law itself."

"I don't agree with that point of view," said K., shaking his head, "for if one accepts it, one must accept as true everything the doorkeeper says. But you yourself have sufficiently proved how impossible it is to do that."

"No," said the priest, "it is not necessary to accept everything as true, one must only accept it as necessary."

"A melancholy conclusion," said K. "It turns lying into a universal principle."

                                                    Franz Kafka

I presume that I am free. I act. the enforcers enforce. I discover that I am not free. then: either I lie (it is necessary to lie) or I struggle (if I do not lie, I must struggle). if I struggle, I ask, why am I not free and what can I do to become free? I wrote this book to find out why I am not free and what I can do to become free.

Though the social structure begins by framing the noblest laws and the loftiest ordinances that "the great of the earth" have devised, in the end it comes to this: breach that lofty law and they take you to a prison cell and shut your human body off from human warmth.

> Ultimately the law is enforced by the unfeeling guard
> punching his fellow man hard in the belly.
>
> Judith Malina

without the presumption of freedom, there is no
freedom. I am free. how, then, do I want to live my
life, do my work, use my body? how, then, do I want to
be, in all my particulars?

standard forms are imposed in dress, behavior,
sexual relation, punctuation. standard forms are imposed on consciousness and behavior — on knowing and
expressing — so that we will not presume freedom, so
that freedom will appear — in all its particulars — impossible and unworkable, so that we will not know what
telling the truth is, so that we will not feel compelled
to tell it, so that we will spend our time and our holy
human energy telling the necessary lies.

standard forms are sometimes called conventions.
conventions are mightier than armies, police, and prisons. each citizen becomes the enforcer, the doorkeeper,
an instrument of the Law, an unfeeling guard punch-
ing his fellow man hard in the belly.

> I am an anarchist. I dont sue, I dont get injunctions, I
> advocate revolution, and when people ask me what
> can we do that's practical, I say, weakly, weaken the
> fabric of the system wherever you can, make possible
> the increase of freedom, all kinds. When I write I
> try to extend the possibilities of expression.
>   . . . I had tried to speak to you honestly, in my own
> way, undisguised, trying to get rid, it's part of my ob-
> ligation to the muse, of the ancien regime of grammar.
>   . . . the revisions in typography and punctuation
> have taken from the voice the difference that distin-

guishes passion from affection and me speaking to
you from me writing an essay.

> Julian Beck, 1965, in a foreword
> to an edition of *The Brig*

BELIEVE THE PUNCTUATION.
Muriel Rukeyser

there is a great deal at stake here. many writers
fight this battle and most lose it. what is at stake for
the writer? freedom of invention. freedom to tell the
truth, in all its particulars. freedom to imagine new
structures.

(the burden of proof is not on those who presume
freedom. the burden of proof is on those who would
in any way diminish it.)

what is at stake for the enforcers, the doorkeepers,
the guardians of the Law — the publishing corporations,
the book reviewers who do not like lower case letters,
the librarians who will not stack books without standard
punctuation (that was the reason given Muriel Rukeyser
when her work was violated) — what is at stake for them?
why do they continue to enforce?

while this book may meet much resistance — anger,
fear, dislike — law? police? courts? — at this moment I
must write: Ive attacked the fundaments of culture.
thats ok. Ive attacked male dominance. thats ok. Ive
attacked every heterosexual notion of relation. thats
ok. Ive in effect advocated the use of drugs. thats ok.
Ive in effect advocated fucking animals. thats ok. here
and now, New York City, spring 1974, among a handful
of people, publisher and editor included, thats ok. lower
case letters are not. it does make one wonder.

so Ive wondered and this is what I think right now. there are well-developed, effective mechanisms for dealing with ideas, no matter how powerful the ideas are. very few ideas are more powerful than the mechanisms for defusing them. standard form — punctuation, typography, then on to academic organization, the rigid ritualistic formulation of ideas, etc. — is the actual distance between the individual (certainly the intellectual individual) and the ideas in a book.

standard form is the distance.

one can be excited *about* ideas without changing at all. one can think *about* ideas, talk *about* ideas, without changing at all. people are willing to think about many things. what people refuse to do, or are not permitted to do, or resist doing, is to change the way they think.

reading a text which violates standard form forces one to change mental sets in order to read. there is no distance. the new form, which is in some ways unfamiliar, forces one to read differently — not to read *about* different things, but to read in different ways.

to permit writers to use forms which violate convention just might permit writers to develop forms which would teach people to think differently: not to think about different things, but to think in different ways. that work is not permitted.

If it had been possible to build the Tower of Babel without ascending it, the work would have been permitted.

Franz Kafka

The Immovable Structure is the villain. Whether that structure calls itself a prison or a school or a fac-

tory or a family or a government or The World As It
Is. That structure asks each man what he can do for it,
not what it can do for him, and for those who do not do
for it, there is the pain of death or imprisonment, or
social degradation, or the loss of animal rights.

Judith Malina

this book is about the Immovable Sexual Structure.
in the process of having it published, Ive encountered
the Immovable Punctuation Typography Structure,
and I now testify, as so many have before me, that the
Immovable Structure aborts freedom, prohibits invention, and does us verifiable harm: it uses our holy human energy to sustain itself; it turns us into enforcers,
or outlaws; to survive, we must learn to lie.

The Revolution, as we live it and as we imagine it,
means destroying the Immovable Structure to create
a world in which we can use our holy human energy to
sustain our holy human lives;

to create a world without enforcers, doorkeepers,
guards, and arbitrary Law;

to create a world — a community on this planet —
where instead of lying to survive, we can tell the truth
and flourish.

NOTES

Chapter 1. Onceuponatime: The Roles

[1] The Brothers Grimm, *Household Stories* (New York: Dover Publications, 1963), p. 213.

[2] *Ibid.*, p. 213.

[3] *Ibid.*, p. 214.

[4] *Ibid.*

[5] *Ibid.*

[6] *Ibid.*

[7] *Ibid.*, p. 216.

[8] *Ibid.*, p. 221.

[9] *Ibid.*

[10] *Ibid.*

[11] *Ibid.*, p. 124.

[12] *Ibid.*, p. 72.

[13] *Ibid.*, p. 73.

[14] *Ibid.*

[15] *Ibid.*, p. 74.

[16] *Ibid.*, p. 85

[17] *Ibid.*, p. 220.

[18] *Ibid.*, p. 85.

[19] *Ibid.*, p. 92.

Chapter 3. Woman as Victim: *Story of O*

[1] *Newsweek,* March 21, 1966, p. 108, unsigned.

[2] Pauline Réage, *Story of O* (New York: Grove Press, 1965), p. xxi.

[3] *Ibid.*, p. 80.

[4] *Ibid.*, p. 93.

[5] *Ibid.*, p. 187.

[6] *Ibid.*, p. 32.

[7] *Ibid.*, p. 106.

[8] Robert S. de Ropp, *Sex Energy: The Sexual Force in Man and Animals* (New York: Dell Publishing Company, 1969), p. 134.

Chapter 4. Woman as Victim: *The Image*

[1] Jean de Berg, *The Image* (New York: Grove Press, 1966), p. 137.

[2] *Ibid.*, p. 19.

[3] *Ibid.*, p. 47.

[4] *Ibid.*

[5] *Ibid.*, p. 10.

[6] *Ibid.*, p. 11.

[7] *Ibid.*, p. 9.

[8] *Ibid.*, p. 42.

[9] Eliphas Levi, *The History of Magic* (London: Rider and Company, 1969), p. 263.

[10] *Ibid.*, p. 265.

[11] Jean de Berg, *op. cit.*, p. 11.

[12] *Ibid.*, p. 135.

[13] *The Essential Lenny Bruce*, ed. John Cohen (New York: Ballantine Books, 1967), pp. 296–97.

Chapter 5. Woman as Victim: *Suck*

[1] *The Essential Lenny Bruce*, ed. John Cohen (New York: Ballantine Books, 1967), p. 245.

[2] Anne Severson and Shelby Kennedy, *I Change I Am the Same* (n.d.).

[3] *Suck 6.*

[4] *Ibid.*

[5] *Suck 4.*

[6] *Ibid.*

[7] *Ibid.*

[8] *Ibid.*

[9] *Ibid.*

[10] *Suck 2.*

[11] *Ibid.*
[12] *Ibid.*
[13] *Ibid.*
[14] *Ibid.*
[15] *Suck 3.*

Chapter 6. Gynocide: Chinese Footbinding

[1] Howard S. Levy, *Chinese Footbinding: The History of a Curious Erotic Custom* (New York: W. Rawls, 1966), p. 39. Mr. Levy's book is the primary source for all the factual, historical information in this chapter.

[2] *Ibid.*, p. 112.
[3] *Ibid.*, pp. 25–26.
[4] *Ibid.*, p. 26.
[5] *Ibid.*, pp. 26–28.
[6] *Ibid.*, p. 141.
[7] *Ibid.*
[8] *Ibid.*, p. 182.
[9] *Ibid.*, p. 89.
[10] *Ibid.*, p. 144.
[11] *Ibid.*, pp. 144–45.

Chapter 7. Gynocide: The Witches

[1] Jules Michelet, *Satanism and Witchcraft* (London: Tandem, 1969), p. 66.

[2] H. R. Hays, *The Dangerous Sex: The Myth of Feminine Evil* (London: Methuen and Co., 1966), p. 111.

[3] Pennethorne Hughes, *Witchcraft* (Harmondsworth: Penguin Books, 1971), p. 63.

[4] *Ibid.*, p. 65.
[5] *Ibid.*, pp. 66–67.
[6] Hays, *op. cit.*, p. 147.

[7] Heinrich Kramer and James Sprenger, *Malleus Maleficarum*, trans. by M. Summers (London: Arrow Books, 1971), pp. 29–30.

[8] *Ibid.*, Table of Contents.
[9] *Ibid.*
[10] *Ibid.*, Preface.
[11] Hughes, *op. cit.*, pp. 183–84.

[12] Kramer and Sprenger, *op. cit.*, p. 123.

[13] *Ibid.*, pp. 114–15.

[14] *Ibid.*, pp. 115–16.

[15] *Ibid.*

[16] *Ibid.*, p. 117.

[17] *Ibid.*, p. 118.

[18] *Ibid.*, pp. 119–21.

[19] *Ibid.*, p. 112.

[20] *Ibid.*, pp. 122–23.

[21] Hays, *op. cit.*, p. 151.

[22] *Ibid.*, p. 153.

[23] *Ibid.*

[24] *Ibid.*, p. 89.

[25] The Holy Bible (Philadelphia: National Bible Press, 1954), p. 8.

[26] Michelet, *op. cit.*, p. 68.

[27] Kramer and Sprenger, *op. cit.*, p. 161.

[28] Hughes, *op. cit.*, pp. 97–98.

[29] Gillian Tindall, *A Handbook on Witches* (New York: Atheneum, 1966), p. 99.

[30] Hughes, *op. cit.*, p. 156.

[31] *Ibid.*, p. 130.

Chapter 8. Androgyny: The Mythological Model

[1] M. Esther Harding, *Woman's Mysteries: Ancient and Modern* (London: Rider and Company, 1971), pp. 35–36.

[2] *Ibid.*, p. 36.

[3] Mircea Eliade, *Myths, Dreams, and Mysteries: The Encounter between Contemporary Faiths and Archaic Realities* (New York: Harper & Row, 1960), p. 23.

[4] *The Secret of the Golden Flower*, introduction by Richard Wilhelm (London: Routledge, 1962), p. 12.

[5] Agehananda Bharati, *The Tantric Tradition* (Garden City: Doubleday and Company, 1970), pp. 18–19.

[6] *Ibid.*, p. 200.

[7] Joseph Campbell, *The Masks of God: Primitive Mythology* (New York: Viking, 1969), p. 109.

[8] *Ibid.*, p. 105.

[9] Joseph Campbell, *The Hero with a Thousand Faces* (Princeton: Princeton University Press, 1968), p. 154.

[10] Midrash, Rabbah, 8:1.
[11] Harding, *op. cit.*, pp. 282–83.

Chapter 9. Androgyny: Androgyny, Fucking, and Community

[1] Mary Jane Sherfey, M.D., *The Nature and Evolution of Female Sexuality* (New York: Vintage Books, 1973), p. 43.

[2] Ann Oakley, *Sex, Gender and Society* (New York: Harper & Row, 1972), p. 24.

[3] Sherfey, *op. cit.*, pp. 50–51.

[4] Oakley, *op. cit.*, p. 30.

[5] Robert T. Francoeur, *Utopian Motherhood: New Trends in Human Reproduction* (Cranbury, N.J.: A. S. Barnes, 1973), p. 139.

[6] Sherfey, *op. cit.*, p. 50.

[7] *Ibid.*, p. 173.

[8] Francoeur, *op. cit.*, p. 139.

[9] *Ibid.*, p. 140.

[10] *Ibid.*

[11] *Ibid.*

[12] *Ibid.*, p. 197.

BIBLIOGRAPHY

Adams, Elsie, and Mary Louise Briscoe, eds. *Up Against the Wall, Mother*. Glencoe Press, 1971.

Andersen, Hans Christian. *The Snow Queen and Other Tales*. New York: New American Library, 1966.

Ariès, Philippe. *Centuries of Childhood: A Social History of Family Life*. New York: Alfred A. Knopf, 1962.

Barber, Benjamin R. *Superman and Common Men: Freedom, Anarchy, and the Revolution*. New York: Praeger, 1971.

Baring-Gould, William S. and Ceil, eds. *The Annotated Mother Goose*. New York: Clarkson N. Potter, 1962.

Barrie, J. M. *Peter Pan*. New York: Scribners, 1950.

Bataille, Georges. *Eroticism*. London: John Calder, 1962.

Bebel, August. *Woman under Socialism*. New York: Schocken Books, 1971.

Beck, Julian. *The Life of the Theatre: The Relation of the Artist to the Struggle of the People*. San Francisco: City Lights, 1972.

Bharati, Agehananda. *The Tantric Tradition*. Garden City: Doubleday and Company, 1970.

Black, Jonathan, ed. *Radical Lawyers: Their Role in the Movement and in the Courts*. New York: Avon Books, 1971.

Blofeld, John. *The Tantric Mysticism of Tibet*. New York: E. P. Dutton, 1970.

Boston Women's Health Book Collective. *Our Bodies, Our Selves: A Book by and for Women*. New York: Simon and Schuster, 1973.

Campbell, Joseph. *The Hero with a Thousand Faces*. Princeton: Princeton University Press, 1968.

———. *The Masks of God: Oriental Mythology*. New York: Viking, 1962.

——. *The Masks of God: Primitive Mythology.* New York: Viking, 1969.

Chadwick, Nora. *The Celts.* Harmondsworth: Penguin Books, 1970.

Churchward, James. *The Lost Continent of Mu.* New York: Paperback Library, 1970.

Clébert, Jean-Paul. *The Gypsies.* Harmondsworth: Penguin Books, 1967.

Cohen, John, ed. *The Essential Lenny Bruce.* New York: Ballantine Books, 1967.

Coon, Carleton S. *The History of Man.* Harmondsworth: Penguin Books, 1967.

Crawley, Ernest. *The Mystic Rose: A Study of Primitive Marriage and of Primitive Thought in Its Bearing on Marriage.* London: Spring Books, 1965.

Davies, R. Trevor. *Four Centuries of Witch Beliefs.* London: Methuen, 1947.

de Berg, Jean. *The Image.* New York: Grove Press, 1966.

De Crow, Karen. *The Young Woman's Guide to Liberation: Alternatives to a Half-Life While the Choice Is Still Yours.* Indianapolis: Bobbs-Merrill, 1971.

Deming, Barbara. "Two Perspectives on Women's Struggle," *Liberation.* Vol. 17, No. 10, pp. 30–38.

de Ropp, Robert S. *Sex Energy: The Sexual Force in Man and Animals.* New York: Dell, 1969.

Dralys, Lord. *The Beautiful Flagellants of New York.* New York: Grove Press, 1971.

Duniway, Abigail Scott. *Pathbreaking: An Autobiographical History of the Equal Suffrage Movement in Pacific Coast States.* New York: Schocken Books, 1971.

Eliade, Mircea. *Myths, Dreams, and Mysteries: The Encounter between Contemporary Faiths and Archaic Realities.* New York: Harper & Row, 1960.

——. *Shamanism: Archaic Techniques of Ecstasy.* Princeton: Princeton University Press, 1964.

Farb, Peter. *Man's Rise to Civilisation.* London: Paladin, 1971.

Ferenczi, Sandor. *Thalassa: A Theory of Genitality.* New York: W. W. Norton, 1968.

Figes, Eva. *Patriarchal Attitudes.* Greenwich, Conn: Fawcett Publications, 1970.

Firestone, Shulamith. *The Dialectic of Sex: The Case for Feminist Revolution.* New York: Bantam Books, 1972.

Fox, Robin. *Kinship and Marriage.* Harmondsworth: Penguin Books, 1967.

Francoeur, Robert T. *Utopian Motherhood: New Trends in Human Reproduction.* Cranbury, N.J.: A. S. Barnes, 1973.

Goldman, Emma. *The Traffic in Women and Other Essays on Feminism.* New York: Times Change Press, 1970.

Goode, William J., ed. *The Contemporary American Family.* Chicago: Quadrangle Books, 1971.

Green, Richard, M.D., and John Money, eds. *Transsexualism and Sex Reassignment.* Baltimore: The Johns Hopkins Press, 1969.

Greenwald, Harold, and Aron Krich, eds. *The Prostitute in Literature.* New York: Ballantine Books, 1960.

Grimm, The Brothers. *Household Stories.* New York: Dover Publications, 1963.

Grogan, Emmett. *Ringolevio: A Life Played for Keeps.* New York: Avon Books, 1972.

Gunkel, Hermann. *The Legends of Genesis: The Biblical Saga and History.* New York: Schocken Books, 1964.

Hamilton, Edith. *Mythology: Timeless Tales of Gods and Heroes.* New York: New American Library, 1959.

Hansen, Chadwick. *Witchcraft at Salem.* New York: New American Library, 1970.

Harding, M. Esther. *Woman's Mysteries: Ancient and Modern.* London: Rider and Company, 1971.

Harrison, Jane Ellen. *Mythology.* New York: Harcourt, Brace and World, 1963.

Hays, H. R. *The Dangerous Sex: The Myth of Feminine Evil.* London: Methuen, 1966.

Heline, Corinne. *Mysteries of the Holy Grail.* San Francisco: New Age Press, 1963.

Hole, Christina. *Witchcraft in England.* London: B. T. Batsford, 1945.

Holzer, Hans. *The Truth about Witchcraft.* Garden City: Doubleday and Company, 1969.

Hughes, Pennethorne. *Witchcraft.* Harmondsworth: Penguin Books, 1971.

Humana, Charles, and Wang Wu. *The Yin Yang: The Chinese Way of Love.* London: Allan Wingate, 1971.

Jacobs, Joseph, compiler. *Celtic Fairy Tales.* New York: Dover Publications, 1968.

———. *English Fairy Tales.* New York: Dover Publications, 1967.

———. *Indian Fairy Tales.* New York: Dover Publications, 1969.

———. *More Celtic Fairy Tales.* New York: Dover Publications, 1968.

Johnston, Jill. *Lesbian Nation: The Feminist Solution.* New York: Simon and Schuster, 1973.

Jung, Carl G., ed. *Man and His Symbols.* New York: Dell Publishing Company, 1971.

Jung, C. G. *Psyche and Symbol.* Edited by Violet S. de Laszlo. Garden City: Doubleday & Anchor, 1958.

Jung, C. G., and C. Kerényi. *Essays on a Science of Mythology: The Myth of the Divine Child and the Mysteries of Eleusis.* Princeton: Princeton University Press, 1969.

Jung, Emma, and Marie-Louise von Franz. *The Grail Legend.* London: Hodder and Stoughton, 1960.

Kanter, Rosabeth Moss. *Commitment and Community: Communes and Utopias in Sociological Perspective.* Cambridge, Mass.: Harvard University Press, 1972.

Kraditor, Aileen S., ed. *Up from the Pedestal: Selected Writings in the History of American Feminism.* Chicago: Quadrangle Books, 1968.

Kramer, Heinrich, and James Sprenger. *Malleus Maleficarum.* Trans. M. Summers. London: Arrow Books, 1971.

Kronhausen, Drs. Phyllis and Eberhard. *Erotic Fantasies: A Study of the Sexual Imagination.* New York: Grove Press, 1969.

Leach, Maria. *The Beginning: Creation Myths around the World.* New York: Funk and Wagnalls, 1956.

Lederer, Wolfgang. *The Fear of Women.* New York: Harcourt Brace Jovanovich, 1968.

Legman, J. *Rationale of the Dirty Joke: An Analysis of Sexual Humor.* New York: Grove Press, 1968.

Lenin, V. I. *The Emancipation of Women.* New York: International Publishers, 1970.

L'Estrange, Ewen C. *Witchcraft and Demonianism.* London: Heath Cranton, 1933.

Lever, Janet and Pepper Schwartz. *Women at Yale: Liberating a College Campus.* Indianapolis: Bobbs-Merrill, 1971.

Levi, Eliphas. *The History of Magic.* London: Rider and Company, 1969.

Levi-Strauss, Claude. *Totemism.* Harmondsworth: Penguin Books, 1963.

Levy, Howard S. *Chinese Footbinding: The History of a Curious Erotic Custom.* New York: W. Rawls, 1966.

Lewis, I. M. *Ecstatic Religion: An Anthropological Study of Spirit,*

Possession, and Shamanism. Harmondsworth: Penguin Books, 1971.

Loth, David. *The Erotic in Literature*. New York: Macfadden-Bartell, 1962.

Lowen, Alexander. *The Betrayal of the Body*. London: Collier-Macmillan, 1967.

Mallet-Joris, Francoise. *The Witches*. New York: Paperback Library, 1970.

Mancini, J. G. *Prostitutes and Their Parasites: An Historical Survey*. London: Elek Books, 1963.

Marcuse, Herbert. *Eros and Civilization: A Philosophical Inquiry into Freud*. New York: Alfred A. Knopf, 1955.

Michelet, Jules. *Satanism and Witchcraft*. London: Tandem, 1969.

Millett, Kate. *Sexual Politics*. Garden City: Doubleday and Company, 1970.

Mitchell, Juliet. *Woman's Estate*. New York: Pantheon, 1971.

Morgan, Robin, ed. *Sisterhood Is Powerful*. New York: Vintage Books, 1970.

Morton, Miriam, ed. *A Harvest of Russian Children's Literature*. Berkeley: University of California Press, 1967.

Murray, Margaret A. *The God of the Witches*. London: Oxford University Press, 1970.

——. *The Witch-Cult in Western Europe*. Oxford: Clarendon Press, 1962.

Neumann, Erich. *The Great Mother: An Analysis of the Archetype*. Trans. Ralph Manheim. Princeton: Princeton University Press, 1963.

Newton, Huey P. *Revolutionary Suicide*. New York: Harcourt Brace Jovanovich, 1973.

Nicholson, Irene. *Mexican and Central American Mythology*. Feltham: Paul Hamlyn, 1967.

Oakley, Anne. *Sex, Gender and Society*. New York: Harper & Row, 1972.

Ostrander, Sheila and Lynn Schroeder. *Psychic Discoveries behind the Iron Curtain*. New York: Bantam Books, 1971.

Peck, Ellen. *The Baby Trap*. New York: Bernard Geis, 1971.

Perrault, Charles. *Classic French Fairy Tales*. New York: Meredith Press, 1967.

The Pillow-Book of Sei-Shōnagon. Trans. Arthur Waley. London: Unwin Books, 1960.

Pyle, Howard. *The Story of the Champions of the Round Table.* New York: Dover Publications, 1968.

The Quest of the Holy Grail. Trans. P. M. Matarasso. Harmondsworth: Penguin Books, 1969.

Rafiq, B. A. *The Status of Women in Islam.* London: The London Mosque, no date.

Réage, Pauline. *Story of O.* New York: Grove Press, 1965.

Redgrove, H. Stanley. *Magic and Mysticism: Studies in Bygone Beliefs.* New York: University Books, 1971.

Reich, Charles A. *The Greening of America.* New York: Random House, 1970.

Reich, Wilhelm. *Character Analysis.* New York: Farrar, Straus and Giroux, 1970.

——. *Listen, Little Man.* New York: Farrar, Straus and Giroux, 1971.

——. *The Function of the Orgasm.* London: Panther Books, 1968.

——. *The Mass Psychology of Fascism.* New York: Farrar, Straus and Giroux, 1970.

Roszak, Betty and Theodore, eds. *Masculine/Feminine: Readings in Sexual Mythology and the Liberation of Women.* New York: Harper & Row, 1969.

Rubin, Jerry. *Do It: Scenarios of the Revolution.* New York: Simon and Schuster, 1970.

Sanders, Ed. *Shards of God: A Novel of the Yippies.* New York: Grove Press, 1971.

Schulder, Diane and Florynce Kennedy. *Abortion Rap.* New York: McGraw-Hill, 1971.

Scott, G. R. *Flagellation: The Story of Corporal Punishment.* London: Tallis Press, 1968.

The Secret of the Golden Flower. Trans. Richard Wilhelm. London: Routledge, 1962.

Seligmann, Kurt. *Magic, Supernaturalism, and Religion.* New York: Universal Library, 1968.

Sherfey, Mary Jane, M.D. *The Nature and Evolution of Female Sexuality.* New York: Vintage Books, 1973.

Skinner, B. F. *Beyond Freedom and Dignity.* New York: Bantam Books, 1972.

Sontag, Susan. *Styles of Radical Will.* New York: Dell, 1970.

Stanton, Elizabeth Cady. *Eighty Years and More: Reminiscences 1815–1897.* New York: Schocken Books, 1971.

Starkey, Marion L. *The Devil in Massachusetts: A Modern Inquiry into the Salem Witch Trials.* Garden City: Doubleday and Company, 1961.

Storr, Anthony. *Human Aggression.* Harmondsworth: Penguin Books, 1968.

Sullerot, Evelyne. *Woman, Society, and Change.* London: World University Library, 1971.

Tanner, Leslie B., ed. *Voices from Women's Liberation.* New York: New American Library, 1971.

Taylor, G. Rattray. *Sex in History.* New York: Ballantine Books, 1954.

Thomas, Keith. *Religion and the Decline of Magic: Studies in Popular Beliefs in 16th and 17th Century England.* London: Weidenfeld and Nicolson, 1971.

Tiger, Lionel. *Men in Groups.* New York: Vintage Books, 1970.

Tindall, Gillian. *A Handbook on Witches.* New York: Atheneum, 1966.

Toch, Hans. *Violent Men: An Inquiry into the Psychology of Violence.* Harmondsworth: Penguin Books, 1972.

Trachtenberg, Joshua. *Jewish Magic and Superstition: A Study in Folk Religion.* New York: Atheneum, 1970.

Trocchi, Alexander. *Helen and Desire.* Chatsworth, Calif.: Brandon House, 1967.

———. *Thongs.* Chatsworth, Calif.: Brandon House, 1967.

Ullerstam, Lars. *The Erotic Minorities: A Swedish View.* London: Calder and Boyars, 1967.

Vermes, Geza. *The Dead Sea Scrolls in English.* Harmondsworth: Penguin Books, 1968.

Violations of the Child Marilyn Monroe. By her psychiatrist-friend. New York: Bridgehead Books, 1962.

Vivas, Eliseo. *Contra Marcuse.* New Rochelle: Arlington House, 1971.

Waite, A. E. *The Holy Kabbalah: A Study of the Secret Tradition in Israel as Unfolded by Sons of the Doctrine for the Benefit and Consolation of the Elect Dispersed through the Lands and Ages of the Greater Exile.* New York: University Books, 1971.

Watts, Alan W. *The Two Hands of God: The Myths of Polarity.* New York: Collier Books, 1963.

Wilson, Colin. *Origins of the Sexual Impulse.* London: Panther Books, 1963.

PERMISSIONS
ACKNOWLEDGMENTS

Grateful acknowledgment is due for permission to quote from the following copyright material:

From Julian Beck, *The Life of the Theatre*. Copyright © 1972 by Julian Beck. Reprinted by permission of City Lights Books.

From Jean de Berg, *The Image*. Copyright © 1966 by Grove Press. Reprinted by permission of Grove Press, Inc.

From Robert T. Francoeur, *Utopian Motherhood*. Copyright © 1970 by Robert T. Francoeur. Reprinted by permission of Doubleday & Company, Inc.

From Heinrich Kramer and James Sprenger, *Malleus Maleficarum*, translated by Montague Summers. Reprinted by permission of the Translator's Literary Estate and The Hogarth Press.

From Howard S. Levy, *Chinese Footbinding: The History of a Curious Erotic Custom*. Reprinted by permission of its publisher Walton H. Rawls, New York, 1966. (Distributed by Twayne Publishers.)

From Pauline Reage, *Story of O*. Copyright © 1965 by Grove Press. Reprinted by permission of Grove Press, Inc.

From Virginia Woolf, *A Room of One's Own*. Copyright © 1929 by Virginia Woolf; renewed 1957 by Harcourt Brace Jovanovich, Inc. Reprinted by permission of the publisher.

RIGHT-WING WOMEN

Andrea Dworkin

'Feminism is hated because women are hated'

Why do some women support Right-wing movements, even though they curtail their freedoms? Andrea Dworkin's timeless, visionary analysis goes to the heart of this contradiction, exploring the Right's positions on abortion, sexuality, racism and antifeminism, and showing how it attempts both to exploit and to quiet women's deepest fears of male violence. The Right-wing woman, Dworkin contends, acquiesces to male authority for protection and some semblance of power: because 'survival depends on it'.

'Groundbreaking' Bella Abzug

PORNOGRAPHY: MEN POSSESSING WOMEN

Andrea Dworkin

'Pornography is the orchestrated destruction of women's bodies and souls … it is war on women'

Pornography, Andrea Dworkin argued in this landmark work, is about power: the power of owning, of money, of sex. It is not merely violence against women, but the essential DNA of male dominance. As images of women's bodies continue to be manipulated and consumed, her searing, fearless critique of pornographic media is more urgent and discomfiting than ever.

'A major text for our time' Adrienne Rich